READING EXPLORER

THIRD EDITION

PAUL MACINTYRE

DAVID BOHLKE

NATIONAL GEOGRAPHIC

LEARNING

Australia · Brazil · Mexico · Singapore · United Kingdom · United States

NATIONAL GEOGRAPHIC
L E A R N I N G

National Geographic Learning,
a Cengage Company

Reading Explorer Split 4A
Third Edition

Paul MacIntyre and David Bohlke

Publisher: Andrew Robinson

Executive Editor: Sean Bermingham

Associate Development Editor: Yvonne Tan

Director of Global Marketing: Ian Martin

Heads of Regional Marketing:

   Charlotte Ellis (Europe, Middle East and Africa)

   Kiel Hamm (Asia)

   Irina Pereyra (Latin America)

Product Marketing Manager: Tracy Bailie

Senior Production Controller: Tan Jin Hock

Associate Media Researcher: Jeffrey Millies

Art Director: Brenda Carmichael

Operations Support: Hayley Chwazik-Gee

Manufacturing Planner: Mary Beth Hennebury

Composition: MPS North America LLC

For permission to use material from this text or product, submit all requests online at **cengage.com/permissions**
Further permissions questions can be emailed to
permissionrequest@cengage.com

Split 4A with Online Workbook:
ISBN-13: 978-0-357-12459-8

Split 4A:
ISBN-13: 978-0-357-12371-3

National Geographic Learning
200 Pier Four Blvd
Boston, MA 02210
USA

Locate your local office at **international.cengage.com/region**

Visit National Geographic Learning online at **ELTNGL.com**
Visit our corporate website at **www.cengage.com**

Printed in China
Print Number: 01   Print Year: 2019

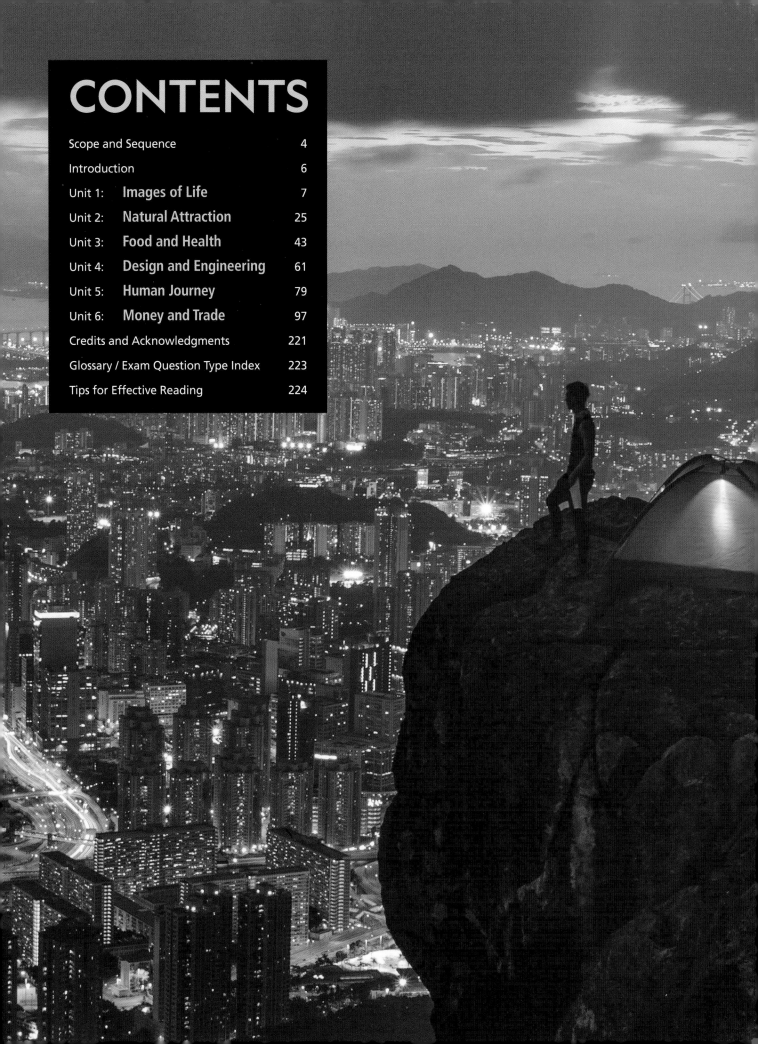

CONTENTS

SCOPE AND SEQUENCE

ACADEMIC SKILLS

READING SKILL	VOCABULARY BUILDING	CRITICAL THINKING
A: Understanding Words with Multiple Meanings **B:** Scanning for Information (1)—Short Answer Questions	**A:** Suffix *-tic* **B:** Synonyms of *thus*	**A:** Evaluating Pros and Cons **B:** Interpreting; Reflecting
A: Summarizing (1)—Using a Concept Map **B:** Identifying Figurative Language	**A:** Word root *scend* **B:** Suffix *-ility*	**A:** Speculating **B:** Interpreting/Applying; Speculating
A: Recognizing Cause and Effect Relationships (1) **B:** Evaluating Arguments	**A:** Suffix *-wide* **B:** Synonyms of *diminish*	**A:** Analyzing Solutions **B:** Evaluating Arguments and Ideas
A: Scanning for Information (2)—Matching Information to Paragraphs **B:** Recognizing Lexical Cohesion	**A:** Collocations with *vital* **B:** Prefix *fore-*	**A:** Applying Ideas **B:** Applying Ideas
A: Synthesizing Information **B:** Distinguishing Fact from Speculation	**A:** Collocations with *rate* **B:** Suffix *-ous*	**A:** Reflecting/Evaluating **B:** Reflecting
A: Understanding the Function of Sentences **B:** Summarizing (2)—Creating an Outline	**A:** Collocations with *policy* **B:** Word usage: *principle* vs. *principal*	**A:** Evaluating Pros and Cons **B:** Reflecting

READING EXPLORER brings the world to your classroom.

With *Reading Explorer* you learn about real people and places, experience the world, and explore topics that matter.

What you'll see in the Third Edition:

Real-world stories give you a better understanding of the world and your place in it.

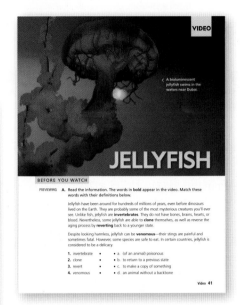

National Geographic Videos expand on the unit topic and give you a chance to apply your language skills.

Reading Skill and **Reading Comprehension** sections provide the tools you need to become an effective reader.

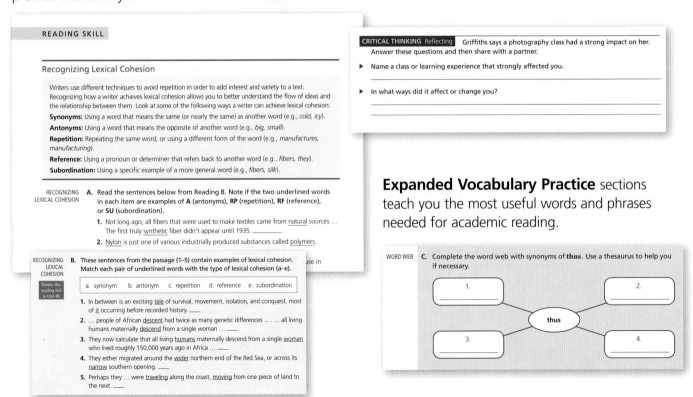

READING SKILL

Recognizing Lexical Cohesion

Writers use different techniques to avoid repetition in order to add interest and variety to a text. Recognizing how a writer achieves lexical cohesion allows you to better understand the flow of ideas and the relationship between them. Look at some of the following ways a writer can achieve lexical cohesion:

Synonyms: Using a word that means the same (or nearly the same) as another word (e.g., *cold, icy*).
Antonyms: Using a word that means the opposite of another word (e.g., *big, small*).
Repetition: Repeating the same word, or using a different form of the word (e.g., *manufactures, manufacturing*).
Reference: Using a pronoun or determiner that refers back to another word (e.g., *fibers, they*).
Subordination: Using a specific example of a more general word (e.g., *fibers, silk*).

RECOGNIZING LEXICAL COHESION **A.** Read the sentences below from Reading B. Note if the two underlined words in each item are examples of **A** (antonyms), **RP** (repetition), **RF** (reference), or **SU** (subordination).

1. Not long ago, all fibers that were used to make textiles came from natural sources … The first truly synthetic fiber didn't appear until 1935. _____
2. Nylon is just one of various industrially produced substances called polymers.

RECOGNIZING LEXICAL COHESION
Review this reading skill in Unit 4B
B. These sentences from the passage (1–5) contain examples of lexical cohesion. Match each pair of underlined words with the type of lexical cohesion (a–e).

| a. synonym | b. antonym | c. repetition | d. reference | e. subordination |

1. In between is an exciting tale of survival, movement, isolation, and conquest, most of it occurring before recorded history. _____
2. … people of African descent had twice as many genetic differences … … all living humans maternally descend from a single woman … _____
3. They now calculate that all living humans maternally descend from a single woman who lived roughly 150,000 years ago in Africa … _____
4. They either migrated around the wider northern end of the Red Sea, or across its narrow southern opening. _____
5. Perhaps they … were traveling along the coast, moving from one piece of land to the next. _____

CRITICAL THINKING Reflecting Griffiths says a photography class had a strong impact on her. Answer these questions and then share with a partner.

▶ Name a class or learning experience that strongly affected you.

▶ In what ways did it affect or change you?

Expanded Vocabulary Practice sections teach you the most useful words and phrases needed for academic reading.

WORD WEB **C.** Complete the word web with synonyms of **thus**. Use a thesaurus to help you if necessary.

1.
2.
thus
3.
4.

IMAGES
OF LIFE

A father and son share a
quiet moment at a mosque
in New Delhi, India.

WARM UP

Discuss these questions with a partner.

1. What kinds of things do you usually
   photograph?

2. What can a photograph do that words
   cannot?

Amateur photographer Haig Gilchrist captures the moment a giant wave hits a ferry near Sydney Harbour, Australia. This dramatic photo was viewed by thousands online.

BEFORE YOU READ

DEFINITIONS **A.** Read the sentence below. Match the correct form of each word in **bold** with its definition (1–3).

In addition to using professional **photojournalists**, many magazines and newspapers today rely on **amateur** photographers to **document** important events.

1. _____ : to record in written or photographic form

2. _____ : working without being paid; not professional

3. _____ : a reporter who shares news using images

SKIMMING **B.** Skim paragraphs A and B. Which of these statements would the author most likely agree with? Circle a, b, or c. Check your answer as you read the passage.

a. The quality of smartphone photos is usually not very good.

b. Smartphones and apps have allowed anyone to be a photographer.

c. Many photojournalists don't approve of amateur photography.

THE VISUAL VILLAGE

A Before the age of the smartphone, aspiring photographers had to learn how to use high-tech cameras and photographic techniques. Not everyone had cameras, and it took skill and a good eye to capture and create a great photograph. Today, with the huge range of camera apps on our smartphones, we are all amateur photographers. And pretty good ones, too: The quality of smartphone images now nearly equals that of digital cameras.

B The new ease of photography has given us a **tremendous** appetite for capturing the magical and the ordinary. We are **obsessed** with documenting everyday moments, whether it's a shot of our breakfast, our cat—or our cat's breakfast. And rather than collect pictures in scrapbooks, we share, like, and comment on them with friends and strangers around the globe.

C Even photojournalists are experimenting with cell phones because their near invisibility makes it easier to capture unguarded moments.[1] The Internet also allows photojournalists to avoid traditional media. They can now act as their own publishers—reaching huge audiences via social media sites such as Instagram. A photograph taken in New York can get a response from someone in Lagos within a second of being uploaded.

D In the past, magazines published unforgettable photos of important people and global events that captured our imaginations. These photos had the power to change public opinion—even the course of history. But if there are fewer memorable images today, it's not because there are fewer good images: It's because there are so many. No one image gets to be special for long.

E Cameras are everywhere—a situation that is transforming the way we experience **dramatic** events. When there are major political events or natural disasters, it is ordinary citizens with cell phones—not photojournalists— who often provide the first news images. Quality still matters, but it's less important than what's **instantly** shared.

F As people everywhere **embrace** photography and the media make use of citizen journalists, professional standards appear to be shifting. In the past, most people trusted photojournalists to accurately **represent** reality. Today, however, digital images can be altered in ways the naked eye might

---

1 Something done in an **unguarded moment** is done when you think no one is watching.

never notice. Any image can be altered to create an "improved" picture of reality. The average viewer is left with no way to assess the accuracy of an image except through trust in a news organization or photographer.

G The question of the accuracy of images gets even trickier when photojournalists start experimenting with camera apps—like Flickr or Instagram—which encourage the use of filters. Images can be colored, brightened, faded, and scratched to make photographs more artistic, or to give them an antique look. Photojournalists using camera apps to cover wars and conflicts have created powerful images—but also **controversy**. Critics worry that antique-looking photographs romanticize war, while distancing us from those who fight in them.

A taxi driver in Kolkata, India, catches up on the news before starting his day (photographed by Annapurna Mellor).

H Yet, photography has always been more subjective than we assume. Each picture is a result of a series of decisions—where to stand, what lens[2] to use, and what to leave in or out of the frame. Does altering photographs with camera app filters make them less true?

---

2 A **lens** is a thin, curved piece of glass or plastic used in things such as cameras.

I There's something powerful and exciting about the experiment that the digital age has forced upon us. These new tools make it easier to tell our own stories, and they give others the power to do the same. Many members of the media get stuck on the same stories, focusing on elections, governments, wars, and disasters. In the process, they miss out on the less dramatic images of daily life that can be just as revealing and **relevant**.

J The increase in the number of photographs and photographers might even be good for **democracy** itself. Hundreds of millions of potential citizen journalists make the world smaller and help keep leaders honest. People can now show what they are up against, making it increasingly difficult for governments to hide their actions. If everyone has a camera, Big Brother[3] isn't the only one watching.

K Who knows? Our obsession with documentation and constantly being connected could lead to a radical change in our way of being. Perhaps we are witnessing the development of a universal visual language. It's one that could change the way we relate to each other and the world. Of course, as with any language, there will be those who produce poetry and those who make shopping lists.

L It's not clear whether this flowering of image-making will lead to a public that better appreciates and understands images. Or will it simply numb[4] us to the **profound** effects a well-made image can have? Regardless, the change is irreversible. Let's hope the millions of new photographs made today help us see what we all have in common, rather than what sets us apart.

---

3 **Big Brother** refers to a person or organization exercising total control over people's lives; the phrase originates from George Orwell's novel *1984*.

4 If an event or experience **numbs** you, you are not able to feel any emotions or think clearly.

A. Choose the best answer for each question.

MAIN IDEA **1.** According to the author, why are there fewer memorable photographs today?

 a. because the quality of many images is very poor
 b. because most images are not interesting to a global audience
 c. because traditional media refuse to publish amateur photos
 (d.) because there are so many good images these days

DETAIL **2.** What kinds of images does the author think matter most these days?

 (a.) images that are important to people and can be shared quickly
 b. high-quality images that help show dramatic events
 c. images presented in a traditional way that reflect reality
 d. images that can be altered to improve one's sense of reality

PURPOSE **3.** Why does the author put the word *improved* in quotation marks in paragraph F?

 a. The writer is using the exact word from another source.
 b. The writer wants to stress that the picture of reality is greatly improved.
 (c.) The writer feels it is questionable whether the picture is truly improved.
 d. The writer is not sure the reader understands the word, so draws attention to it.

INFERENCE **4.** Who does the author criticize in paragraph J?

 a. citizen journalists   c. Big Brother
 b. government leaders   d. people who alter photos

PARAPHRASE **5.** When referring to visual language, what does the author mean by *as with any language, there will be those who produce poetry and those who make shopping lists* (paragraph K)?

 a. It will be most useful for shopping and for writing beautiful poetry.
 b. It will be better because it can be used for a variety of things.
 c. Visual language has certain limitations compared to written language.
 d. Some people will use it for everyday things, and others for more creative things.

MAIN IDEA **B. Match each paragraph with its main idea (a–e).**

 1. Paragraph A   a. More photojournalists are taking smartphone images now and uploading them to social media sites.

 2. Paragraph C   b. The effect on us of the increasing number of photographs is still uncertain.

 3. Paragraph E   c. When there are big or dramatic news stories, amateur photographers often share the first images with the public.

 4. Paragraph G   d. Altering photos with camera apps can give viewers a misleading impression about serious events such as wars.

 5. Paragraph L   e. Anyone can be an amateur photographer now because photos taken on smartphones are almost as good as photos taken on digital cameras.

Understanding Words with Multiple Meanings

Many words have more than one meaning. In some cases, the words may be different parts of speech; for example, a noun and a verb. They may be different in meaning (e.g., a **slip** of paper, to **slip** on the ice), or similar (e.g., to score a **goal**, my **goal** in life). In each case, you may need to use a dictionary to understand a word's exact meaning.

IDENTIFYING MEANING
A. Scan paragraphs A–D in Reading A to find the words in bold below (1–6). Then choose the correct meaning (a or b) for each.

1. **age**   (a.) a period in history   b. how old someone is
2. **pretty**   (a.) quite   b. attractive
3. **appetite** a. physical hunger   (b.) a strong desire
4. **act**   a. an action   (b.) to behave
5. **second**   (a.) a 60th of a minute   b. number two in a series
6. **course**   a. a class   (b.) the direction

ANALYZING
B. Read each of these excerpts from Reading A (1–4). Choose the sentence in which the underlined word has the same meaning as the bold word.

1. … makes it easier to **capture** unguarded moments. (paragraph C)

    a. NASA is using space telescopes to help <u>capture</u> images of distant planets.
    b. The <u>capture</u> of the gang's leader should lead to less crime in the city.

2. Photojournalists using camera apps to **cover** wars … (paragraph G)

    a. The local media will <u>cover</u> the results of the election.
    b. His photo appeared on the <u>cover</u> of a magazine.

3. … a result of a **series** of decisions … (paragraph H)

    a. There has been an unusual <u>series</u> of events.
    b. What is the most popular comic book <u>series</u>?   *trilogy*

4. … and what to leave in or out of the **frame**. (paragraph H)

    a. It looked like somebody was trying to <u>frame</u> him for the theft.
    b. Look in the camera <u>frame</u> and tell me what you see.

CRITICAL THINKING Evaluating Pros and Cons   Do you think news photographers should be allowed to use filters when publishing images of serious subjects (e.g., wars)? What are the pros and cons of doing so? Discuss with a partner and note your ideas.

Pros: _____

Cons: _____

Your opinion: _____

COMPLETION **A.** Circle the correct words to complete the paragraph below.

Recent years have seen some ¹**relevant / dramatic** changes in photography. The availability of cell phones has allowed millions of people to ²**embrace / represent** photography as a hobby. Image-sharing apps allow anyone to share photos ³**instantly / profoundly** with friends and followers online; some people become ⁴**tremendous / obsessed** with capturing and documenting every detail of their lives. However, the popularity of image-sharing sites has also raised some ⁵**obsessive / controversial** issues—for example, when images of an individual are widely shared without the person's knowledge.

WORDS IN CONTEXT **B.** Complete each sentence with the correct answer (a or b).

1. A **controversy** involves _____ among people.
   a. agreement
   b. disagreement

2. If a photo **represents** a place, it _____ what the place is like.
   a. shows
   b. doesn't show

3. In a **democracy**, citizens _____ the right to vote.
   a. have
   b. don't have

4. If the ideas in an old book are **relevant** today, they _____ matter.
   a. no longer
   b. still

5. If you feel a **tremendous** amount of pressure, you feel _____ of pressure.
   a. a lot
   b. a little bit

6. Something that is **profound** is felt or experienced very _____.
   a. briefly
   b. strongly

WORD FORMS **C.** We can add *-tic* to some nouns to form adjectives (e.g., *drama* + *-tic* = **dramatic**). Complete the sentences below using the adjectives in the box.

athletic	democratic	dramatic	genetic

1. A person's _____ ability—for example, their speed and strength—may be partly affected by _____ factors.

2. In the 20th century, many countries held their first _____ elections.

3. In 2011, Amy Weston took a(n) _____ photo of a woman leaping to safety from a burning building.

DEFINITIONS **A.** You are going to read about photographer Annie Griffiths. Below are some expressions she uses (1–5). What do you think they mean? Match each one with its definition (a–e).

1. small talk   •   • a. light conversation

2. put at ease   •   • b. addicted; obsessed

3. hooked   •   • c. make people feel comfortable

4. by some miracle •   • d. extremely good; excellent

5. top-notch   •   • e. amazingly; surprisingly

PREDICTING **B.** What could be some challenges of being a professional photographer? Discuss with a partner. Then check your ideas as you read the passage.

Annie Griffiths has photographed in nearly 150 countries during her career.

MY JOURNEY IN PHOTOGRAPHS

BY ANNIE GRIFFITHS

> An Omani fisherman casts his net at dawn.

A   I got my first real job at age 12, as a waitress. I am convinced that I learned more as a waitress than I ever did in a classroom. When I went on to college, it also paid for **tuition** and housing and—eventually—a camera. But best of all, being a waitress taught me to quickly assess and understand all kinds of people. I learned how to make small talk and how to quickly put people at ease—great training for a journalist. Waiting tables also taught me **teamwork** and service and humor.

B   From the moment I picked up a camera, I was hooked. I lost interest in other studies, and all I wanted to do was take pictures for the university newspaper, the *Minnesota Daily*. In six months, I was able to get a lot of great experience. The week I finished college, I was contacted by the *Worthington Daily Globe*, a regional daily newspaper in southern Minnesota with a history of excellence in photography. By some miracle I was hired, and the two-year experience that followed was like a master class in photojournalism.

C   Jim Vance was the top-notch publisher of the *Globe*. He had very high **expectations** of all the staff. With little or no instruction from him, writers and photographers were expected to fill the paper with stories that were important to our readers. I didn't know it at the time, but this independent reporting was perfect training for my future career.

D   Among the most important things I learned at the *Globe* was that if you can make friends with a shy Norwegian farmer and be invited to his kitchen table, you can probably do well in any culture on Earth. I worked with a wonderful writer named Paul Gruchow. Together we would search the farming communities for stories. Paul had grown up on a farm himself and lived through personal tragedy, so he was able to **project** warmth and understanding to anyone he met. Farmers would invite us into their homes and willingly share their personal thoughts with us. From Paul I learned how to be a patient listener, as well as the importance of giving each subject time and **sincere** attention.

A portrait of an Indian woman from a poor background who became a solar engineer

E It was while I was working at the *Globe* that I happened to answer the phone one morning. A man's voice asked, "You a photographer?" When I replied that indeed I was, the voice responded, "This is Bob Gilka. *National Geographic*. I need a hail[1] damage picture. You guys get a big hailstorm last night?" I **overcame** my nervousness and said, "Yes, sir." When he asked if I could take the picture for him, I again said, "Yes, sir."

F My little picture of hail damage in southern Minnesota was well received, and a year later, I was working for Bob—*National Geographic*'s legendary director of photography. **Thus** began one of the most important relationships of my life.

Lessons on the Road

G I was the youngest photographer working for *National Geographic* when I arrived in 1978, and I spent at least a decade just trying not to make mistakes. With each new assignment came the fear that this was going to be the one where they figured out that I couldn't do the job.

H On many assignments, the most challenging part **turned out** to be the transportation. Over the years, I traveled by horse, car, train, truck, and all sorts of old vehicles. I traveled by mule[2] in Mexico, by ship along the Indian Ocean, by fishing boat in the Sea of Galilee, by moped[3] in Bermuda, by sailboat in Sydney. I flew in helicopters chasing bears in the Arctic. Twice, while flying in light planes, pilots have had to make emergency landings far from any airport. But there were also wonderful experiences. In Africa I traveled by balloon, ultralight aircraft, and elephant. In a rubber raft off the west coast of Mexico, I was suddenly lifted out of the water on the back of a friendly whale.

I Wherever I traveled in the world, taking beautiful pictures was always my goal. However, later in my career, I also wanted my pictures to make a real difference in people's lives. That is why each spring I tour two or three developing countries, shooting **portraits** of people whose lives are better because of the dedicated workers who care about them. The photos are used in a variety of fund-raising products. The other issue that stole my heart was the environment. With support from the National Geographic Expeditions Council, I have traveled all over the United States to photograph the last one percent of wilderness left here.

J I am deeply grateful for my life in photography and the amazing lessons it has taught me. I have learned that women really do hold up half the sky; that language isn't always necessary, but touch usually is; that all people are not alike, but they do mostly have the same hopes and fears; that judging others does great harm, but listening to them **enriches**; and that it is impossible to hate a group of people once you get to know one of them as an individual.

---

1 **Hail** is small balls of ice that fall from the sky like rain.
2 A **mule** is a hybrid between a horse and a donkey.
3 A **moped** is a type of lightweight motorcycle.

A. Choose the best answer for each question.

PURPOSE   *b* **1.** What is the purpose of paragraph A?

    a. to show how working as a waitress is similar to life as a photographer

    b. to explain how Griffiths' first job helped prepare her for her future career

    c. to compare Griffiths' life before and after being a waitress

    d. to describe how Griffiths became interested in photography at college

SEQUENCE   *c* **2.** What happened after Griffiths graduated from college?

    a. She picked up a camera for the first time.

    b. She began working at the *Minnesota Daily*.

    c. She got a job at the *Worthington Daily Globe*.

    d. She started teaching photography.

DETAIL   *a* **3.** Which sentence does NOT describe Griffiths' job at the *Globe*?

    a. She received detailed instructions from her publisher.

    b. She learned how to be a patient listener.

    c. The experience prepared her well for a job at *National Geographic*.

    d. She was expected to fill the paper with stories that readers wanted.

DETAIL   *c* **4.** What kind of transportation challenge does Griffiths mention?

    a. having an accident in a fishing boat

    b. getting attacked by an elephant

    c. being forced to land in a remote place

    d. getting lost in the ocean in a rubber raft

MAIN IDEA   *d* **5.** According to Griffiths, what has life as a photographer taught her?

    a. that language is essential for communication

    b. that most people have very different hopes and fears

    c. that expressing an opinion is as important as listening

    d. that it is important to get to know people as individuals

IDENTIFYING MEANING

Review this reading skill in Unit 1A

B. Scan the section "Lessons on the Road" to find the words in **bold** below (1–6). Then choose the correct meaning (a or b) for each.

1. spent   a. paid money for something   (b) passed time in a specific way

2. light   (a.) not heavy   b. pale; not dark

3. back   (a.) rear surface of a body   b. in the opposite direction

4. spring   a. to suddenly jump forward   (b) the season after winter

5. left   a. went away   (b) remaining

6. once   a. one time only   (b) as soon as; when

Scanning for Information (1)—Short Answer Questions

Scanning is an important skill for taking exams, but how you approach scanning should depend on the question type. With **short answer questions**, for example, read each question carefully first to determine the information you need. Check if there is a word limit for each answer. Identify key words in the questions, and think about what synonyms might be in the text. Then scan to find the relevant parts of the text. Note that answers normally follow the order they appear in the text.

ANALYZING **A.** Read the questions below. What kind of answer will you need to scan for? Circle a, b, or c.

1. What kind of photographic equipment did Griffiths' waitress job help pay for?

   a. an object b. a number c. a reason

2. For how long was Griffiths employed at the *Worthington Daily Globe*?

   a. a place b. a specific date c. a time period

3. What was Bob Gilka's role at *National Geographic*?

   a. a person's name b. a place c. a job title

4. Where did Griffiths travel by moped?

   a. a reason b. a place c. a number

5. Why did Griffiths' goals change later in her career?

   a. an example b. an activity c. a reason

SCANNING **B.** Scan Reading B and write short answers to the questions above.

1. _____
2. _____
3. _____
4. _____
5. _____

CRITICAL THINKING Interpreting

▶ Griffiths says she has learned that "women really do hold up half the sky." What do you think she means by this? Discuss with a partner.

▶ What examples can you think of that support her statement? Note some ideas below. Then share them with a partner.

_____
_____
_____

VOCABULARY PRACTICE

COMPLETION **A.** Circle the correct words to complete the paragraph below.

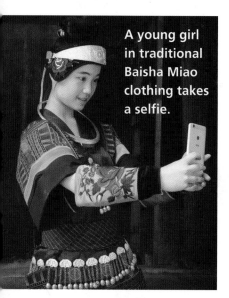

A young girl in traditional Baisha Miao clothing takes a selfie.

There are a few things to keep in mind when taking a selfie. First, think about what emotion you want to convey. For example, do you want the photo to ¹**turn out / project** love, sadness, or joy? Do you want it to look natural or perhaps more formal and posed? Decide on your location, and try different angles and distances. Experiment with different camera features. Remember, though, that while new technologies may ²**enrich / overcome** your photo, you might prefer a simpler ³**portrait / tuition**, even one in black and white. How your final selfie ⁴**overcomes / turns out** will ⁵**thus / portrait** depend on a number of factors.

DEFINITIONS **B.** Match the words in the box with the definitions below.

enrich	expectation	overcome
sincere	teamwork	tuition

1. _____ : to successfully deal with a problem
2. _____ : a belief that someone will or should achieve something
3. _____ : honest; not pretending or lying
4. _____ : payment for instruction, especially in a college or university
5. _____ : the effort of people working together to get something done
6. _____ : to improve or make better

WORD WEB **C.** Complete the word web with synonyms of **thus**. Use a thesaurus to help you if necessary.

1. _____

2. _____

thus

3. _____

4. _____

University students in Dubai, photographed by Annie Griffiths

A PHOTOGRAPHER'S LIFE

BEFORE YOU WATCH

DISCUSSION

A. You are going to watch an interview with Annie Griffiths. Discuss these questions with a partner.

1. Based on the information in Reading B and the photo above, what kinds of photos do you think Griffiths likes to take?

2. What do you think Griffiths hopes to achieve with her photography?

PREDICTING

B. Read these extracts from the video. What words do you think are missing? Discuss with a partner and complete the sentences with your guesses. Use one word for each blank.

"I think our kids also understand that people all over the world are [1]_____ — that you don't assume that they are going to be the same as we are. But then if you go into each culture open, and look [2]_____ in the eye, and observe and [3]_____, you're going to make [4]_____ ..."

"[Photography is] a wonderful, terrible job because you get this [5]_____ to go out and do it, but then you're supposed to do it [6]_____ than it's ever been done before."

GIST **A.** Watch the video. Check your guesses in Before You Watch B. Are they correct or similar to what Annie Griffiths says in the video?

MULTIPLE CHOICE **B.** Watch the video again. Choose the correct answer for each question.

1. What did Griffiths want to be before she got interested in photography?

   a. a writer
   b. a painter

2. What benefit did Griffiths' daughter gain from the family's travels?

   a. She can speak several languages.
   b. She is now a confident traveler.

3. What tip does Griffiths give for immersing yourself in a different culture?

   a. staying away from tourist hotspots
   b. respecting the local way of life

4. According to Griffiths, what is one of the most inspirational parts about photography?

   a. It gives you the opportunity to be creative and grow artistically.
   b. A good photo can help shape or change public opinion.

CRITICAL THINKING Reflecting   Griffiths says a photography class had a strong impact on her. Answer these questions and then share with a partner.

▶ Name a class or learning experience that strongly affected you.

_____

▶ In what ways did it affect or change you?

_____

_____

VOCABULARY REVIEW

Do you remember the meanings of these words? Check (✓) the ones you know. Look back at the unit and review any words you're not sure of.

Reading A

☐ controversy*   ☐ democracy   ☐ dramatic*   ☐ embrace   ☐ instantly

☐ obsessed   ☐ profound   ☐ relevant*   ☐ represent   ☐ tremendous

Reading B

☐ enrich   ☐ expectation   ☐ overcome   ☐ portrait   ☐ project*

☐ sincere   ☐ teamwork   ☐ thus   ☐ tuition   ☐ turn out

* Academic Word List

NATURAL ATTRACTION

Discuss these questions with a partner.

1. Which animals are known for their bright colors or spectacular appearance?

2. In what ways do you think those characteristics help the animals?

∧ The Victoria crowned pigeon is known for its large head crest of lacy feathers.

2A

BEFORE YOU READ

DISCUSSION **A.** Read the information below. What types of animals do you know that are bioluminescent? Make a list.

Bioluminescence is the production and emission of light by living organisms, through chemical reactions occurring inside their bodies. Simply put, creatures that are bioluminescent can glow in the dark. Examples of bioluminescent creatures can be found in the ocean, on land, and in the air.

PREDICTING **B.** Why might it be useful for an organism to be bioluminescent? Brainstorm some purposes with a partner. Check your ideas as you read the passage.

> The bioluminescent bay on the Puerto Rican island of Vieques

LIVING
LIGHT

A The ability of some species to create light—known as bioluminescence—is both magical and commonplace. Magical, because of its glimmering beauty. Commonplace, because many life forms can do it. On land the most familiar examples are fireflies, **flashing** to attract mates on a warm summer night. But there are other luminous land organisms, including glow-worms, millipedes, and some 90 species of fungus. Even some birds, such as the Atlantic puffin, have beaks that glow in the dark.

B But the real biological light show takes place in the sea. Here, an **astonishing** number of beings can make light. Some, such as ostracods, are like ocean fireflies, using flashes of light to attract a mate. There are also glowing bacteria, and light-making fish, squid, and jellyfish. Indeed, of all the groups of organisms known to make light, more than four-fifths live in the ocean.

C As a place to live, the ocean has a couple of peculiarities. Firstly, there is almost nowhere to hide, so being **invisible** is very important. Secondly, as you **descend**, sunlight disappears. At first, red light is absorbed. Then the yellow and green parts of the spectrum disappear, leaving just the blue. At 200 meters below the surface, the ocean becomes a kind of perpetual twilight,[1] and at 600 meters the blue fades out too. In fact, most of the ocean is as black as the night sky. These **factors** make light uniquely useful as a weapon or a veil.

Hiding with Light

D In the ocean's upper **layers**, where light penetrates, creatures need to blend in to survive. Any life form that stands out is in danger of being spotted by **predators**—especially those swimming below, looking up. Many life forms solve this problem by avoiding the light zone during the day. Others—such as jellyfish and swimming snails—are **transparent**, ghostlike creatures, almost impossible to see.

E Other sea species use light to survive in the upper layers—but how? Some, such as certain shrimp and squid, illuminate their bellies to match the light coming from above. This allows them to become invisible to predators below. Their light can be turned on and off at will—some even have a dimmer switch.[2] For example, certain types of shrimp can alter how much light they give off, depending on the brightness of the water around them. If a cloud passes overhead and briefly blocks the light, the shrimp will dim itself accordingly.

F But if the aim is to remain invisible, why do some creatures light up when they are touched, or when the water nearby is **disturbed**? A couple of reasons. First, a sudden burst of light may startle[3] a predator, giving the prey a chance to escape. Some kinds of deep-sea squid, for example, give a big squirt of light before darting off into the gloom.

G Second, there is the principle of "the enemy of my enemy is my friend." Giving off light can help summon the predator of your predator. Known as the "burglar alarm" effect, this is especially useful for tiny life forms, such as dinoflagellates, that cannot swim fast. For such small beings, water is too viscous[4] to allow a quick getaway—it would be like trying to swim through syrup. Instead, when threatened by a shrimp, for example, these organisms light up. The flashes attract larger fish that are better able to spot—and eat—the shrimp. The chief defense for these tiny organisms is therefore not fight or flight—but light.

---

1 **Twilight** is the time of day after the sun sets but before it becomes completely dark.

2 A **dimmer switch** is a device—such as those found on lamps—that can control the brightness of a light.

3 If something **startles** you, it causes you to feel surprised or shocked.

4 A liquid that is **viscous** is thick and not easy to move through.

5 **Flagella** are thin, threadlike structures that enable tiny organisms such as bacteria or protozoa to swim.

STARS OF THE SEA

One of the best places in the world to see a natural light show is Vieques, a small island that belongs to Puerto Rico. The island is famous for its *bahía bioluminiscente,* or "bio bay"—home to **countless** dinoflagellates. These dust-size beings are named for their two flagella[5] and the whirling motion they make (*dinos* means "whirling" in Greek). Dinoflagellates light up whenever the water around them moves; they are the organisms typically responsible for the flashes of light you sometimes see when swimming or boating on a dark night.

Visitors to Vieques can join an evening tour group and set out across the bay in transparent canoes. The island has only a few streetlights, so when the moon is not yet risen, the sea is dark and the sky is full of stars. Fish dart through the water, looking like meteors. Eventually, the movement of the canoes disturbs the dinoflagellates, and they light up in a bright, flickering stream. Watching them through the canoe's transparent floor can give a powerful impression that the water is part of the sky, and you are paddling through the stars.

▽ **Examples of bioluminescence in the natural world include (1) the comb jelly, (2) the firefly, (3) squid, and (4) some species of mushroom.**

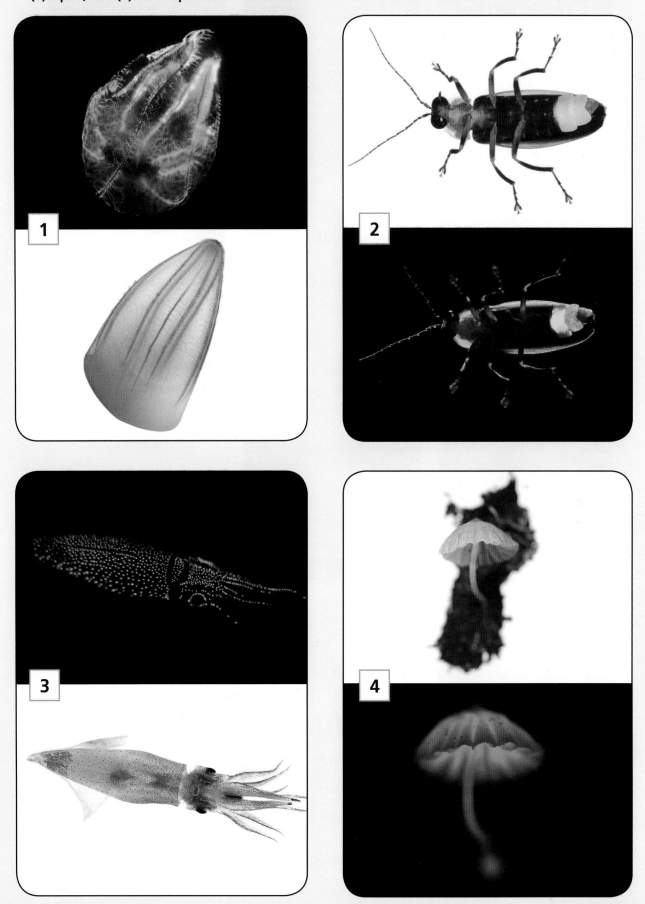

DEFENSE

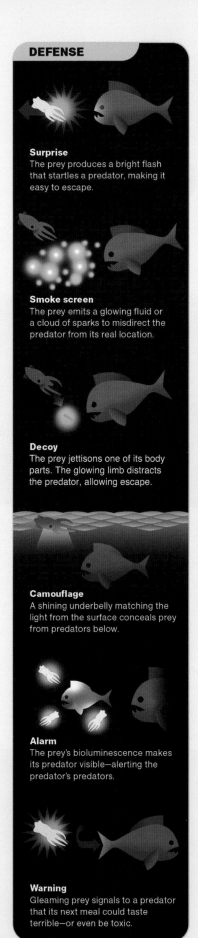

Surprise
The prey produces a bright flash that startles a predator, making it easy to escape.

Smoke screen
The prey emits a glowing fluid or a cloud of sparks to misdirect the predator from its real location.

Decoy
The prey jettisons one of its body parts. The glowing limb distracts the predator, allowing escape.

Camouflage
A shining underbelly matching the light from the surface conceals prey from predators below.

Alarm
The prey's bioluminescence makes its predator visible—alerting the predator's predators.

Warning
Gleaming prey signals to a predator that its next meal could taste terrible—or even be toxic.

OFFENSE

Shock
A burst of bright light from a bioluminescent predator stuns prey and leaves it open to attack.

Lure
Prey is attracted to the glow produced by a predator.

Beacon
Predators seek out the glimmer that tells them that bioluminescent creatures are gathering.

Searchlight
A predator turns on its natural spotlight to locate prey in a dark ocean.

REPRODUCTION

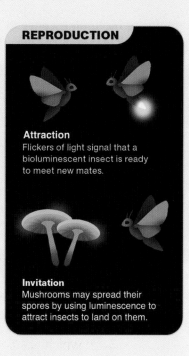

Attraction
Flickers of light signal that a bioluminescent insect is ready to meet new mates.

Invitation
Mushrooms may spread their spores by using luminescence to attract insects to land on them.

Lightness of Being

Glow-in-the-dark light may seem mysterious, but organisms use it for practical purposes. Bioluminescence warns off predators, lures prey, and attracts mates. Making light is such a useful trait that it has evolved independently at least 40 times, for three main reasons.

JASON TREAT, NGM STAFF. ART: ELEANOR LUTZ
SOURCE: STEVEN HADDOCK, MONTEREY BAY AQUARIUM RESEARCH INSTITUTE

A. Choose the best answer for each question.

MAIN IDEA *b* **1.** All life forms with bioluminescence _____ .

    a. live in or near water

    b. are able to create light

    c. use light to attract mates

    d. use light to protect themselves

DETAIL *c* **2.** Which of these is NOT explained in the passage?

    a. why some bioluminescent creatures produce light

    b. why invisibility is important to many sea creatures

    c. why some birds have beaks that glow in the dark

    d. how various creatures near the ocean's surface hide themselves

COHESION *c* **3.** In which position should this sentence be added to paragraph D?
These creatures only rise toward the surface at night.

    a. after the first sentence

    b. after the second sentence

    c. after the third sentence

    d. after the fourth sentence

DETAIL / SYNTHESIZING *b* **4.** According to paragraph E, how do certain shrimp in the ocean's upper layers use bioluminescence?

    a. as a decoy   c. as an alarm

    b. as camouflage   d. as a warning

INFERENCE *d* **5.** What is meant by the "burglar alarm" effect?

    a. Light allows predators to spot their prey in total darkness.

    b. A sudden flash of light startles predators, allowing their prey to escape.

    c. When lit up, tiny organisms such as dinoflagellates can swim faster.

    d. Organisms produce light, which attracts the predators of their predators.

EVALUATING STATEMENTS **B.** Are the following statements true or false according to the reading passage, or is the information not given? Circle **T** (true), **F** (false), or **NG** (not given).

1. Most bioluminescent creatures in the sea live near the surface.   T F **(NG)**

2. Six hundred meters below the surface, sunlight stops penetrating the ocean.   **(T)** F NG

3. Dinoflagellates use light to help them find and eat shrimp.   T **(F)** NG

4. Human activity in the Vieques "bio bay" stops dinoflagellates from lighting up.   T **(F)** NG

5. Visitors to the Vieques "bio bay" can only see dinoflagellates in the summer.   T F **(NG)**

Summarizing (1)—Using a Concept Map

To help you identify and remember a passage's key ideas, it can be useful to take notes using a concept map. This allows you to see the relationships and connections between the writer's main and supporting ideas. To create a concept map, start with the main topic in the middle, add subtopics around it, and then list supporting details and examples for each subtopic.

SUMMARIZING **A.** Complete the concept map below with words from Reading A.

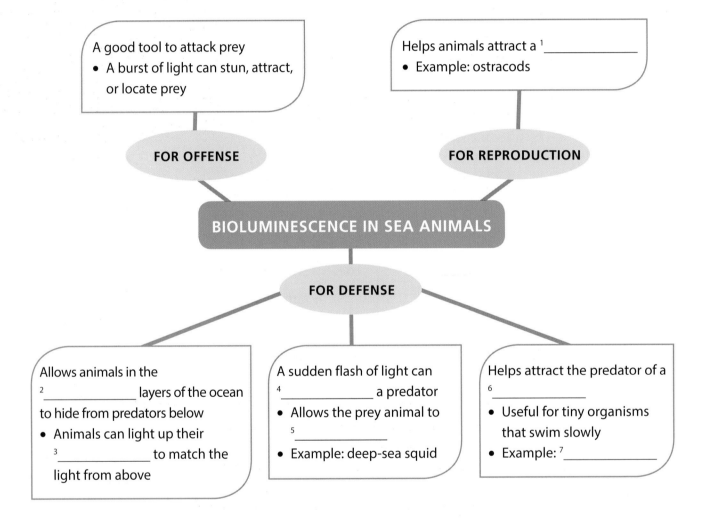

A good tool to attack prey
- A burst of light can stun, attract, or locate prey

Helps animals attract a ¹_____
- Example: ostracods

FOR OFFENSE

FOR REPRODUCTION

BIOLUMINESCENCE IN SEA ANIMALS

FOR DEFENSE

Allows animals in the ²_____ layers of the ocean to hide from predators below
- Animals can light up their ³_____ to match the light from above

A sudden flash of light can ⁴_____ a predator
- Allows the prey animal to ⁵_____
- Example: deep-sea squid

Helps attract the predator of a ⁶_____
- Useful for tiny organisms that swim slowly
- Example: ⁷_____

CRITICAL THINKING Speculating   The reading passage mentions that Atlantic puffins have beaks that glow in the dark. What do you think is the purpose of the glowing beak? Discuss with a partner.

> **A puffin beak glows under a black light.**

COMPLETION **A. Circle the correct words to complete the information below.**

A(n) ¹**astonishing** / **disturbed** variety of sea creatures use bioluminescence. Brittle stars, for example, can ²**flash** / **descend** a green light when they are threatened by ³**layers** / **predators**. Some brittle stars can even detach their arms. Predators are attracted to the detached, glowing arm of the brittle star, giving the animal a chance to escape. It later regrows its arm.

Some species of sea cucumber can attach their body parts onto other animals. When frightened or ⁴**transparent** / **disturbed**, these sea cucumbers break off the bioluminescent parts of their bodies onto nearby fish. The predator will follow the glow on the fish, while the sea cucumber simply crawls away.

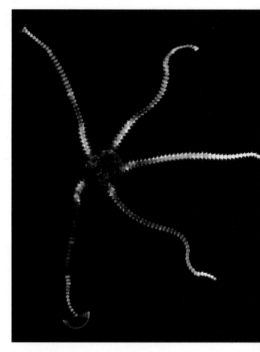

⌃ **Brittle stars are closely related to starfish.**

WORDS IN CONTEXT **B. Complete the sentences. Circle the correct words.**

1. When you **descend** a staircase, you go *up* / *down*.

2. If something is **transparent**, you *can* / *cannot* see through it.

3. Something described as **countless** has a very *low* / *high* number.

4. A **factor** is something that *is unlikely* / *affects a result*.

5. The purpose of adding a **layer** of clothing would likely be to get *warmer* / *wetter*.

6. If something is **invisible**, it *can* / *cannot* be seen.

WORD ROOTS **C. The word descend contains the word root *scend*, which means "move toward." Complete the sentences with the correct words from the box.**

ascend	crescendo	descend	transcend

1. The plane began to _____ as it approached its destination.

2. Divers must not _____ too quickly to the water's surface.

3. Musical symphonies often include a series of softer melodies that build toward a powerful _____ .

4. Some types of music are able to _____ cultural boundaries and become popular worldwide.

DISCUSSION **A.** Look at the photo below. In what way(s) is this bird unusual? Discuss your ideas with a partner.

SKIMMING **B.** Look at the reading title and headings on the next three pages. Check (✓) the information about birds of paradise you think will be covered in the passage. Then read the passage to check your answers.

☐ a. why they have colorful feathers   ☐ c. their migration patterns
☐ b. how they show off their feathers   ☐ d. threats to their survival

∧ A male Wilson's
bird of paradise

FEATHERS OF LOVE

A Covered in soft, black feathers, the **noble** performer bows deeply to his audience. From the top of his head grow several long feathers that tap the ground as he begins his dance. This dancing bird is Carola's parotia, just one of the many birds of paradise that live on the island of New Guinea. This male bird is attempting to impress a row of females that are watching him from a branch above.

B Keeping the females' attention isn't easy. He pauses for dramatic effect, then **commences** his dance again. His neck sinks and his head goes up and down, head feathers **bouncing**. He jumps and shakes his feathers until his performance finally attracts the attention of one of the females.

An Amazing Performance

C In the dense jungle of New Guinea is nature's most **absurd** theater, the special mating game of the birds of paradise. To attract females, males' feathers resemble costumes worthy of the stage. The bright reds, yellows, and blues stand out sharply against the green of the forest. It seems that the more extreme the male's costume and colors, the better his chance of attracting a mate.

D In addition to having extremely beautiful feathers, each species has its own type of display behavior. Some dance on the ground, in areas that they have cleared and prepared like their own version of a dance floor. Others perform high in the trees.

E The male red bird of paradise shows off his red and yellow feathers in a display called a "butterfly dance." He spreads and moves his wings intensely, like a giant butterfly. The male Carola's parotia, however, is the dance king of the birds of paradise; he has serious dance moves! These include one in which he spreads out his feathers like a dress, in a move called the "ballerina[1] dance." While some birds of paradise perform alone, others perform in groups, creating an eye-catching performance that female birds find impossible to resist. Hanging from nearby branches, male Goldie's birds **prominently** display the soft red feathers that rise from their backs as they flap[2] their wings. Excited females soon choose the one that pleased them the most.

The Evolution of Color

F These brilliantly colored birds of paradise have developed over millions of years from ancient birds whose feathers were dark and boring in comparison. Of today's 45 brightly colored birds of paradise species, most live only on New Guinea. These birds of paradise invite us to solve a mystery of nature. It seems to be a contradiction[3] that such extreme feathers and colors could have been favored by the process of **evolution**. After all, these same brightly colored feathers that attract mates also make the birds much more noticeable to predators. The answer lies in the safe environment in which the birds live, and a process of evolution known as sexual selection.

---

1 A **ballerina** is a female ballet dancer.
2 If a bird or an insect **flaps** its wings, the wings move quickly up and down.
3 If an aspect of a situation is a **contradiction**, it is completely different from other aspects and makes the situation confusing.

G "Life here is pretty comfortable for birds of paradise. The island's unique environment has allowed them to go to extremes unheard of elsewhere," says biologist Ed Scholes. Under **harsher** conditions, he says, "evolution simply wouldn't have come up with these birds." Fruit and insects are abundant all year round, and predators are few. The result is a perfect environment for birds.

H Sexual selection has thus been the driving force in the evolution of birds of paradise. Freed of other pressures, birds of paradise began to specialize in attracting mates. Over millions of years, they have slowly **undergone** changes in their colors, feathers, and other talents. Characteristics that made one bird more attractive than another were passed on

and enhanced over time. "The usual rules of survival aren't as important here as the rules of successful mating," Scholes adds.

I The diversity of New Guinea's birds also springs from its varied environments: from coastal plains to cloud forests, from swamps[4] to mountains rising as high as 5,000 meters. The landscape has many physical barriers that isolate animal populations, allowing them to develop into distinct species.

---

4 A **swamp** is an area of very wet land with wild plants growing in it.

> The island of New Guinea is home to nearly 40 species of birds of paradise, more than anywhere else in the world. Most live within a single mountain range and altitude. This isolation allows the birds to evolve separately into their wonderful varieties.

3,000 m

Stephanie's astrapia (*Astrapia stephaniae*)

Brown sicklebill (*Epimachus meyeri*)

King of Saxony bird of paradise (*Pteridophora alberti*)

2,000 m

Superb bird of paradise (*Lophorina superba*)

Western parotia (*Parotia sefilata*)

Buff-tailed sicklebill (*Drepanornis albertisi*)

1,000 m

Raggiana bird of paradise (*Paradisaea raggiana*)

Magnificent bird of paradise (*Cicinnurus magnificus*)

Magnificent riflebird (*Ptiloris magnificus*)

Twelve-wired bird of paradise (*Seleucidis melanoleuca*)

King bird of paradise (*Cicinnurus regius*)

ART BY JOHN NORTON
SOURCES: CLIFFORD B. FRITH, BRUCE M. BEEHLER

Trouble in Paradise

J The people of New Guinea have been watching the displays of the birds of paradise for centuries. "Locals will tell you they went into the forest and copied their **rituals** from the birds," says anthropologist Gillian Gillison. At local dance performances, the painted dancers still evoke the birds with their movements and beautiful costumes. "By wearing the feathers," Gillison says, "... you capture the animal's life force."

K In the past, demand for the birds' feathers resulted in a huge amount of hunting. At the peak of the trade in the early 1900s, 80,000 skins a year were exported from New Guinea for European ladies' hats. Nowadays, few birds die for fashion or for traditional costumes: Ceremonial feathers are passed down from generation to generation. Although local people are still permitted to hunt the birds for traditional uses, they usually target older male birds, leaving younger males to continue **breeding**.

L There are more serious threats to the birds, however. An illegal market in feathers still exists. Large farms use up thousands of hectares of forest where birds of paradise once lived. Logging,[5] oil prospecting, and mining also present dangers to New Guinea's forests. Meanwhile, human populations continue to grow.

M David Mitchell, a conservationist, is relying on the help of local villagers to record where the birds display and what they eat. He hopes to not only gather data, but also encourage protection of the birds' habitat. The strategy seems to be working. "I had come to cut down some trees and plant yam[6] vines," says Ambrose Joseph, one of Mitchell's farmers. "Then I saw the birds land there, so I left the trees alone." For millions of years, these impressive birds have danced to find their mates. They'll keep dancing for as long as the forest offers them a stage.

---

5 **Logging** is the business of cutting down trees for use as wood.

6 A **yam** is a root vegetable, like a potato, that grows in tropical areas.

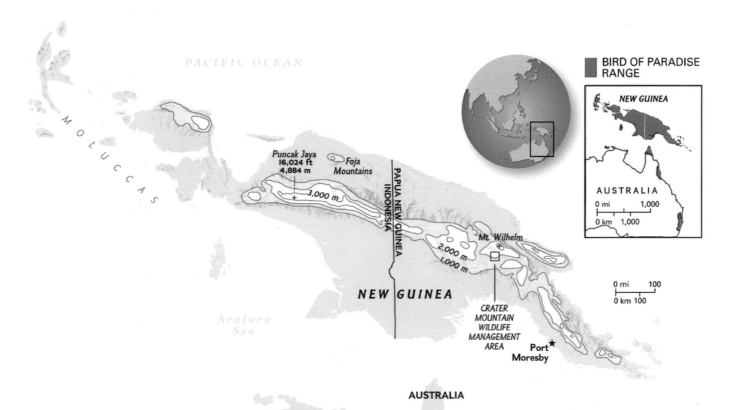

A. Choose the best answer for each question.

MAIN IDEA

1. Why do birds of paradise dance and display their feathers?

a. to frighten away predators

b. to attract a mate

c. to exercise and clean their bodies

d. to show possession of an area

DETAIL

2. Which factor is NOT mentioned as a reason for the birds' unusual characteristics?

a. the widespread availability of fruit and insects

b. the wide variety of environments

c. the wide variety of breeding systems

d. the lack of predators

CAUSE AND EFFECT

3. Why did so many birds of paradise die in the early 1900s?

a. There was a high demand for feathers to use in European hats.

b. The birds got sick after early interactions with humans.

c. Industrial development destroyed the birds' habitat.

d. Logging drastically reduced the birds' habitat.

INFERENCE

4. Why do local people continue to hunt birds of paradise?

a. to eat them

b. to protect smaller birds

c. to make traditional costumes

d. to keep their numbers down

COHESION

5. The following sentence would best be placed at the beginning of which paragraph? *However, there may be some good news for the birds.*

a. paragraph E

b. paragraph I

c. paragraph L

d. paragraph M

IDENTIFYING MEANING

Review this reading skill in Unit 1A

B. Scan the reading passage to find the words in bold below. Then choose the correct meaning (a or b) for each.

1. **bows** (paragraph A)

a. loops or knots

b. bends body forward

2. **row** (paragraph A)

a. a number of things in a line

b. a noisy argument or fight

3. **stage** (paragraph C)

a. a place where people perform

b. a period or part of an activity

4. **display** (paragraph D)

a. to make visible

b. an event or performance meant to entertain

5. **present** (paragraph L)

a. a gift

b. to cause something

Identifying Figurative Language

Writers use figurative language—similes, metaphors, and personification—to create an image of someone or something in the reader's mind.

A **simile** compares two different things using *like* or *as*: *Her skin was as cold as ice.*
A **metaphor** says one thing *is* another thing: *During rush hour, the road is a parking lot.*
Sometimes the comparison in a metaphor is implied: *He has a heart of stone.*
Personification gives humanlike qualities to something nonhuman: *Lightning danced across the sky.*

IDENTIFYING
FIGURATIVE
LANGUAGE

A. Look at these sentences from Reading B. Mark each one as an example of a simile (**S**), a metaphor (**M**), or personification (**P**). Some may have more than one answer.

1. _____ Covered in soft, black feathers, the noble performer bows deeply to his audience. (paragraph A)

2. _____ He spreads and moves his wings intensely, like a giant butterfly. (paragraph E)

3. _____ The male Carola's parotia, however, is the dance king of the birds of paradise. (paragraph E)

4. _____ These include one in which he spreads out his feathers like a dress. (paragraph E)

5. _____ They'll keep dancing for as long as the forest offers them a stage. (paragraph M)

IDENTIFYING
FIGURATIVE
LANGUAGE

B. Look back at Reading A ("Living Light"). Underline these examples of figurative language (1–5) in the passage.

1. A simile in paragraph C

2. A metaphor in paragraph E

3. A simile in paragraph G

4. A simile in the sidebar "Stars of the Sea" (second paragraph)

5. A metaphor in the sidebar "Stars of the Sea" (second paragraph)

CRITICAL THINKING Interpreting / Applying

▶ What does each example of figurative language in activity B mean? What is the writer emphasizing? Discuss with a partner.

▶ Think of some similes or metaphors you could use to describe someone you know. Note your ideas below and then share with a partner.

_____

_____

COMPLETION **A.** Complete the paragraph using the correct form of words from the box.

absurd	bounce	prominent	ritual

Over the years, the male Carola's parotia bird of paradise has developed a special mating [1]_____ that involves a lot of bowing and flapping. On its head, the bird has several long and [2]_____ quills, which it [3]_____ up and down in hopes of attracting a female. "Its mating dance is so [4]_____," says researcher Jennifer Holland, "that I could hardly keep from laughing."

A male parotia dances to attract a female companion.

DEFINITIONS **B.** Match the words in the box with the definitions below.

evolution	breed	commence	noble	harsh	undergo

1. _____ : (for animals) to mate and have babies
2. _____ : to begin
3. _____ : to experience something necessary or unpleasant
4. _____ : cruel or severe
5. _____ : having fine personal qualities or appearance
6. _____ : the way in which living things change and develop over millions of years

WORD FORMS **C.** We can add *-ility* to some adjectives to form nouns (e.g., **noble** + *-ility* = *nobility*). Complete the sentences below with the correct form of words from the box. One word is extra.

hostile	mobile	noble	reliable	stable

1. Economic development is more likely to occur during periods of political _____.

2. Oil is not a _____ energy source in the long term, as supplies are limited.

3. Communication breakdowns can produce a _____ environment in the workplace.

4. The widespread availability of cars in the 20th century led to an increase in personal _____.

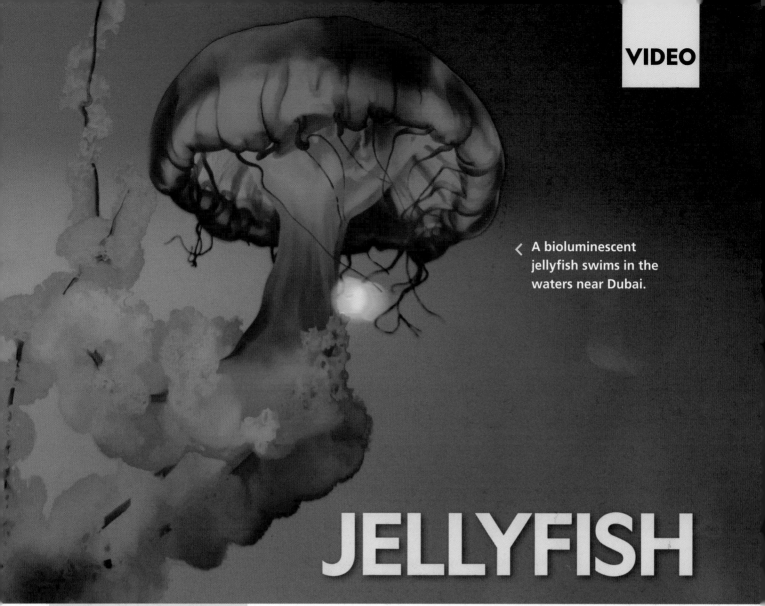

A bioluminescent jellyfish swims in the waters near Dubai.

JELLYFISH

BEFORE YOU WATCH

PREVIEWING

A. Read the information. The words in **bold** appear in the video. Match these words with their definitions below.

Jellyfish have been around for hundreds of millions of years, even before dinosaurs lived on the Earth. They are probably some of the most mysterious creatures you'll ever see. Unlike fish, jellyfish are **invertebrates**. They do not have bones, brains, hearts, or blood. Nevertheless, some jellyfish are able to **clone** themselves, as well as reverse the aging process by **reverting** back to a younger state.

Despite looking harmless, jellyfish can be **venomous**—their stings are painful and sometimes fatal. However, some species are safe to eat. In certain countries, jellyfish is considered to be a delicacy.

1. invertebrate   •   • a. (of an animal) poisonous

2. clone   •   • b. to return to a previous state

3. revert   •   • c. to make a copy of something

4. venomous   •   • d. an animal without a backbone

WHILE YOU WATCH

GIST **A.** Watch the video. Check (✓) the topics that are covered in the video.

- ☐ a. how the jellyfish got its name
- ☐ b. the diet of a jellyfish
- ☐ c. how jellyfish reproduce
- ☐ d. what jellyfish taste like
- ☐ e. problems that large groups of jellyfish can cause

COMPLETION **B.** Watch the video again and complete the notes below. Use up to two words for each blank.

Interesting facts about jellyfish

- Since jellyfish aren't actually fish, some scientists have started using the umbrella term 1"_____" instead.

- By undergoing transdifferentiation, the "immortal jellyfish" can revert back to a 2_____ and start its life cycle all over again.

- The Australian box jellyfish is considered to be the most 3_____ marine animal in the world.

- Jellyfish are mostly made of 4_____; if a jellyfish washes ashore, it will mostly 5_____.

- Jellyfish blooms have clogged fishing gear, destroyed ships, and closed 6_____.

CRITICAL THINKING Speculating   Some jellyfish are bioluminescent. How might this ability be useful to them? Refer to the infographic on page 30 for ideas and discuss with a partner.

VOCABULARY REVIEW

Do you remember the meanings of these words? Check (✓) the ones you know. Look back at the unit and review any words you're not sure of.

Reading A

☐ astonishing	☐ countless	☐ descend	☐ disturb	☐ factor*
☐ flash	☐ invisible*	☐ layer*	☐ predator	☐ transparent

Reading B

☐ absurd	☐ bounce	☐ breed	☐ commence*	☐ evolution*
☐ harsh	☐ noble	☐ prominently	☐ ritual	☐ undergo*

* Academic Word List

FOOD AND HEALTH

3

A woman collects tomatoes in a greenhouse in the Netherlands.

WARM UP

Discuss these questions with a partner.

1. What kinds of foods can be dangerous to your health?

2. In what ways could the world increase its supply of food?

43

BEFORE YOU READ

DEFINITIONS
A. Read this information and match each word or phrase in **bold** with its definition (1–4).

In recent years, **bacteria** found in foods are posing increased health risks— particularly to people with weakened **immune systems**. While improvements in **sanitary** practices have reduced some **foodborne** threats, new hazards have arisen because of changes in our lifestyle and in food production methods.

1. _____ : clean and not dangerous for your health

2. _____ : very small organisms that can cause disease

3. _____ : parts and processes of the body that fight illness

4. _____ : carried into our bodies through the things we eat

PREDICTING
B. What causes food poisoning, and how can we avoid it? Discuss with a partner. Then check your ideas as you read the passage.

HOW SAFE
IS OUR FOOD?

∧ Students study new techniques of food production at Wageningen University & Research, Netherlands.

A The everyday activity of eating involves more risk than you might think. It is estimated that each year in the United States, 48 million people suffer from foodborne diseases; 128,000 of them are hospitalized, and 3,000 die. In the developing world, **contaminated** food and water kill over half a million children a year. In most cases, virulent[1] types of bacteria are to blame.

B Bacteria are an **integral** part of a healthy life. There are 200 times as many bacteria in the intestines[2] of a single human as there are human beings who have ever lived. Most of these bacteria help with **digestion**, making vitamins, shaping the immune system, and keeping us healthy. Nearly all raw food has bacteria in it as well. But the bacteria that produce foodborne illnesses are of a different, more dangerous kind.

Bad Bacteria

C Many of the bacteria that produce foodborne illnesses are present in the intestines of the animals we raise for food. When a food animal containing dangerous bacteria is cut open during processing, bacteria inside can contaminate the meat. Fruits and vegetables can pick up dangerous bacteria if washed or watered with contaminated water. A single bacterium, given the right conditions, divides rapidly enough to produce billions over the course of a day. This means that even only lightly contaminated food can be dangerous. Bacteria can also hide and multiply on dishtowels, cutting boards, sinks, knives, and kitchen counters, where they're easily transferred to food or hands.

D Changes in the way in which farm animals are raised also affect the rate at which dangerous bacteria can spread. In the name of efficiency and economy, fish, cattle, and chickens are raised in giant "factory" farms, which **confine** large numbers of animals in tight spaces. Cattle, for example, are crowded together under such conditions that if only one animal is contaminated with the virulent bacteria *E. coli* O157:H7, it will likely spread to others.

Tracking the Source

E Disease investigators, like Patricia Griffin, are working to find the sources of these outbreaks[3] and prevent them in the future. Griffin, of the Centers for Disease Control and Prevention (CDC) in the United States, has worked in

---

1 Something that is **virulent** is dangerous or poisonous.
2 Your **intestines** are the tubes in your body through which food passes when it has left your stomach.
3 If there is an **outbreak** of something unpleasant, such as violence or a disease, it happens suddenly.

∧ A medical researcher examines a sample of *E. coli*.

the foodborne-disease business for 15 years. Periodic *E. coli* outbreaks turned her attention to the public food safety threat that exists in restaurants and in the food production system. Food safety is no longer just a question of handling food properly in the domestic kitchen. "Now," Griffin says, "we are more aware that the responsibility does not rest solely with the cook. We know that contamination often occurs early in the production process—at steps on the way from farm or field or fishing ground to market."

F Griffin's job is to look for trends in food-related illness through the analysis of outbreaks. Her team tries to identify both the food source of an outbreak and the contaminating bacteria. To link cases together, the scientists use a powerful tool called PulseNet, a national computer network of health laboratories that matches types of bacteria using DNA[4] analysis. PulseNet allows scientists to associate an illness in California, say, with one in Texas, tying together what might otherwise appear as unrelated cases. Then it's the job of the investigators to **determine** what went wrong in the food's journey to the table. This helps them decide whether to recall[5] a particular food or to change the process by which it's produced.

G In January 2000, public health officials in the state of Virginia noted an unusual group of patients sick with food poisoning from salmonella.[6] Using PulseNet, the CDC identified 79 patients in 13 states who were **infected** with the same type of salmonella bacteria. Fifteen had been hospitalized; two had died. What was the common factor? All had eaten mangoes during the previous November and December. The investigation led to a single large mango farm in Brazil, where it was discovered that mangoes were being washed

in contaminated water containing a type of salmonella bacteria. Salmonella contamination is a widespread problem; salmonella cases involving contaminated chicken, melons, coconut, and cereals were reported in 2018.

H The mango outbreak had a larger lesson: We no longer eat only food that is in season or that is grown locally. Instead, we demand our strawberries, peaches, mangoes, and lettuce year-round. As a result, we are depending more and more on imports. Eating food grown elsewhere in the world means depending on the soil, water, and sanitary conditions in those places, and on the way in which their workers farm, harvest, process, and transport the food.

Reducing the Risk

I There are a number of success stories that provide hope and show us how international food production need not mean increased risk of contamination. Costa Rica has made sanitary production of fruits and vegetables a **nationwide** priority. Fresh fruits and vegetables are packed carefully in sanitary conditions; frequent hand washing is **compulsory**; and proper toilets are provided for workers in the fields. Such changes have made Carmela Velazquez, a food scientist from the University of Costa Rica, **optimistic** about the future. "The farmers we've trained," she says, "will become models for all our growers."

J In Sweden, too, progress has been made in reducing the number of foodborne disease at an early stage. Swedish chicken farmers have eliminated salmonella from their farms by thoroughly cleaning the area where their chickens are kept, and by using chicken feed that has been heated to rid it of dangerous bacteria. Consequently, the chickens that Swedes buy are now salmonella-free. These successes suggest that it is indeed **feasible** for companies and farms to produce safe and sanitary food, while still making a profit.

---

4 **DNA** is a material in living things that contains the code for their structure and many of their functions.

5 When sellers **recall** a product, they ask customers to return it to them.

6 **Salmonella** is a group of bacteria that cause food poisoning.

A. Choose the best answer for each question.

GIST
1. What is the reading mainly about?

  a. new research regarding the effects of foodborne bacteria
  b. the decline in sanitary conditions in restaurants and farms around the world
  c. sources of dangerous foodborne bacteria, their detection, and control
  d. the importance of advanced technology in the fight against foodborne bacteria

DETAIL
2. Why is even a single disease-causing bacterium dangerous?

  a. It can mix with other bacteria.
  b. It is often hard to detect.
  c. Just one can kill a small child.
  d. It can multiply very quickly.

PURPOSE
3. What is PulseNet used for?

  a. to match cases of foodborne illness that have the same source
  b. to identify restaurants with poor sanitary conditions
  c. to connect patients who have foodborne illnesses with doctors
  d. to record best practices in food production methods

DETAIL
4. According to the passage, why are people eating more imported food now?

  a. People want to have certain foods year-round.
  b. Imported foods are usually cheaper.
  c. Imported foods are usually safer.
  d. Consumers have more sophisticated tastes.

PARAPHRASE
5. What does Carmela Velazquez mean in paragraph I when she says, "The farmers we've trained will become models for all our growers"?

  a. The farmers will go on TV to talk about what they learned from her.
  b. More farmers will adopt the habits that were taught to the trained farmers.
  c. Both farmers and growers will now work together to assure food safety.
  d. Farmers need to listen to the growers to learn and decide what works for them.

EVALUATING STATEMENTS
B. Are the following statements true or false according to paragraph G, or is the information not given? Circle T (true), F (false), or NG (not given).

1. The salmonella outbreak in 2000 first affected people in Virginia.　　　　**T　F　NG**

2. Everyone affected by that outbreak had eaten mangoes in the previous months.　　　　**T　F　NG**

3. The outbreak was investigated by the Centers for Disease Control and Prevention.　　　　**T　F　NG**

4. The salmonella outbreak was caused by farmers not washing their mangoes.　　　　**T　F　NG**

5. Salmonella can contaminate several different kinds of food.　　　　**T　F　NG**

Recognizing Cause and Effect Relationships (1)

A cause is an action or a condition that makes something happen. An effect is a result of that action. Some texts use words that indicate cause and effect relationships, such as *caused*, *as a result*, *because (of)*, *so*, *due to*, *consequently*, *thus*, and *the reason*. In other cases, a writer may imply a cause-effect relationship without using these words. As you read, try to make connections between events by asking *What caused …?* and *What was the result of …?* questions.

ANALYZING **A.** Read the sentences below. In each sentence, underline the cause.

1. I didn't go to the doctor because I forgot about the appointment.
2. The medicine in our cabinet was old, so we threw it out.
3. The reason I didn't go to school was that I had a stomachache.
4. Due to new health guidelines, all food will be removed from the staff fridge on weekends.
5. Investigators believe improper hand washing caused the disease outbreak at the school.

CAUSE AND EFFECT **B.** Match each cause below with its effect according to information from Reading A.

Causes

1. cutting open a food animal during processing •
2. the use of "factory" farms •
3. a salmonella outbreak linked to mangoes •
4. all-year demand for fresh fruits and vegetables •
5. improving sanitary conditions on farms •

Effects

• a. fewer cases of contaminated produce
• b. the death of two people
• c. meat can be contaminated by the bacteria inside
• d. greater dependence on imports
• e. bacteria will likely spread from animal to animal

CRITICAL THINKING Analyzing Solutions   Discuss these questions with a partner.

▶ How have Costa Rica and Sweden reduced the occurrence of foodborne diseases? Complete these notes with information from the reading passage.

Costa Rica: focus on safer farming of _____

Sweden: focus on safer farming of _____

▶ What might be some of the challenges of each approach? Note your ideas below.

_____

_____

VOCABULARY PRACTICE

DEFINITIONS **A.** Read the information below. Match each word in **red** with its definition (1–6).

In 2008, **contaminated** food caused a scare in the United States. Nine people died and 700 people **nationwide** suffered **infection** from salmonella poisoning. Authorities **determined** that the cause of the salmonella outbreak was peanut products.

Peanuts are used in a wide variety of products and are an **integral** part of health bars, cookies, ice cream varieties, and even dog biscuits. Although officials couldn't order a **compulsory** recall, stores voluntarily removed peanut products from their shelves.

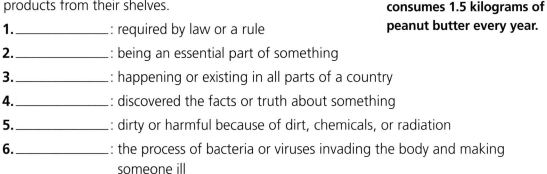

⌃ The average American consumes 1.5 kilograms of peanut butter every year.

1. ＿＿＿＿＿＿＿＿: required by law or a rule
2. ＿＿＿＿＿＿＿＿: being an essential part of something
3. ＿＿＿＿＿＿＿＿: happening or existing in all parts of a country
4. ＿＿＿＿＿＿＿＿: discovered the facts or truth about something
5. ＿＿＿＿＿＿＿＿: dirty or harmful because of dirt, chemicals, or radiation
6. ＿＿＿＿＿＿＿＿: the process of bacteria or viruses invading the body and making someone ill

WORDS IN CONTEXT **B.** Complete each sentence with the correct answer (a or b).

1. If contamination is **confined**, it ＿＿＿＿＿＿.
   a. occurs within a certain area   b. has spread to many areas

2. **Digestion** is the body's system of ＿＿＿＿＿＿.
   a. fighting disease   b. breaking down food

3. If a project is **feasible**, it ＿＿＿＿＿＿ be done.
   a. can   b. cannot

4. An **optimistic** person believes that the future will be ＿＿＿＿＿＿ than today.
   a. worse   b. better

WORD PARTS **C.** The suffix *-wide* in **nationwide** means "extending throughout." Complete the sentences using the words in the box. One word is extra.

city	company	nation	world

1. The outbreak was confined to the U.S.; it affected 12 states ＿＿＿＿**wide**.
2. Shanghai has implemented a ＿＿＿＿**wide** smoking ban in all its public parks.
3. Affecting millions of people ＿＿＿＿**wide**, malaria is particularly prevalent in tropical countries.

BEFORE YOU READ

DISCUSSION **A.** Read the information below. What risks might be associated with biotech foods? Discuss with a partner.

In recent years, scientists have discovered ways of altering the genes of foods. For example, corn can be changed genetically so it's more resistant to insects, diseases, and droughts. While these biotech foods seem to offer clear benefits, critics say there are risks of genetically altering our food.

PREDICTING **B.** Read the questions below. Discuss your answers with a partner. Then read the passage to check your ideas.

1. Are biotech foods safe for humans?

2. Can biotech foods harm the environment?

3. Can biotech foods help feed the world?

The eggplants on the right have been genetically altered to increase insect resistance.

THE BATTLE FOR BIOTECH

A Genetic engineering (GE) of crops and animals through the manipulation of DNA is producing a **revolution** in food production. The potential to improve the quality and **nutritional** value of the food we eat seems unlimited. Such potential benefits **notwithstanding**, critics fear that genetically engineered products—so-called biotech foods—are being rushed to market before their effects are fully understood.

Q: What exactly are biotech foods?

B Biotech foods are produced from animals and plants that have been genetically altered. Genetic alteration is nothing new. Humans have been altering the genetic **traits** of plants for thousands of years by keeping seeds from the best crops and planting them the following years, and by breeding varieties to

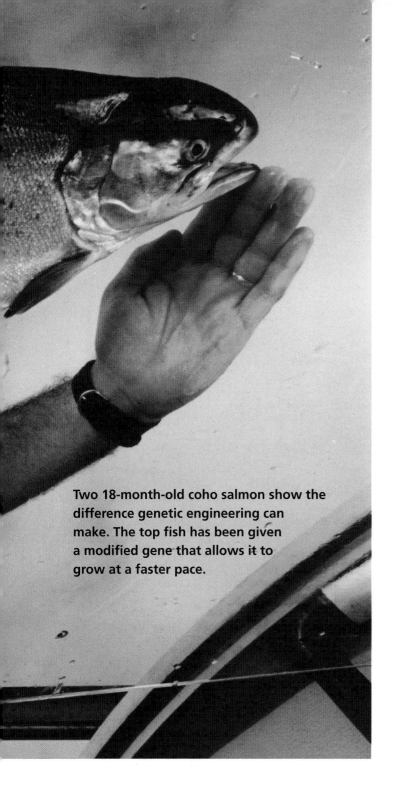

Two 18-month-old coho salmon show the difference genetic engineering can make. The top fish has been given a modified gene that allows it to grow at a faster pace.

make them taste sweeter, grow bigger, or last longer. In this way, we've transformed the wild tomato from a fruit the size of a small stone to the giant ones we have today.

C   On the other hand, the techniques of genetic engineering are new and different. **Conventional** breeders always used plants or animals that were related, or genetically similar. In so doing, they transferred tens of thousands of genes. In contrast, today's genetic engineers can transfer just a few genes at a time between species that are distantly related, or not related at all. There are surprising examples: Rat genes have been inserted into lettuce plants to make a plant that produces vitamin C. Moth genes have been inserted into apple trees to add disease resistance. The purpose of conventional and modern techniques is the same—to insert genes from an organism that carries a desired trait into one that does not. Several dozen biotech food crops are currently on the market, among them varieties of corn, soybeans, and cotton. Most of these crops are engineered to help farmers deal with common farming problems such as weeds,[1] insects, and disease.

Q: Are biotech foods safe for humans?

D   As far as we know. So far, problems have been few. In fact, according to a 2016 report from the National Academy of Sciences in the United States, "No differences have been found that indicate a higher risk to human health and safety from these GE foods than from their non-GE counterparts." Some GE foods might even be safer than non-GE foods. Corn damaged by insects often contains high levels of fumonisins—toxins[2] that grow in the wounds of the damaged corn. Lab tests have linked fumonisins with cancer in animals. Studies show that most corn **modified** for insect resistance has lower levels of fumonisins than conventional corn damaged by insects.

E   However, biotech foods have had problems in the past. One such problem occurred in the mid-1990s, when soybeans were modified using genes from a nut. The

---

1 A **weed** is a wild plant that prevents other plants from growing properly.
2 A **toxin** is any poisonous substance produced by bacteria, animals, or plants.

TYPE AND LOCATION OF GE CROPS, 2015

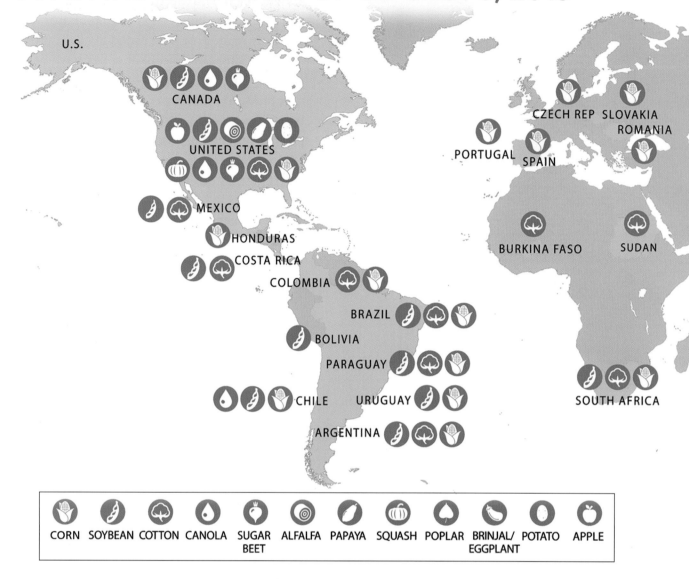

| CORN | SOYBEAN | COTTON | CANOLA | SUGAR BEET | ALFALFA | PAPAYA | SQUASH | POPLAR | BRINJAL/ EGGPLANT | POTATO | APPLE |

modified soybeans contained a protein[3] that causes reactions in humans who are **allergic** to nuts. While this protein was discovered before any damage was done, critics fear that other harmful proteins created through genetic modification may slip by unnoticed. Moving genes across dramatically different species—such as rats and lettuce—also makes critics nervous. They fear something could go wrong either in the function of the inserted gene or in the function of the host[4] DNA, with the possibility of unexpected health effects.

---

3 **Protein** is a substance found in food like meat and eggs.

4 A **host** is an animal or plant in which a foreign organism lives.

5 **Pesticides** are chemicals used to kill harmful insects.

Q: Can biotech foods harm the environment?

F Most scientists agree that the main safety issues of GE crops involve not people but the environment. Allison Snow, a plant ecologist at Ohio State University, worries that GE crops are being developed too quickly and released before they've been adequately tested.

G On the other hand, advocates of GE crops argue that some genetically modified plants may actually be good for the land, by offering an environmentally friendly **alternative** to pesticides,[5] which can pollute water and harm animals. Far fewer pesticides need to

and many other scientists argue that genetic modification can help address the urgent problems of food shortage and hunger by increasing crop quantities. Crops can be engineered to grow in areas with harsh, dry climates or in soils not usually suitable for farming.

I According to the World Health Organization, an estimated 250 million children in the world suffer from vitamin A **deficiency**. Between 250,000 and 500,000 go blind every year as a result, with half of those children dying within a year of losing their sight. "Golden rice"—a biotech variety named for its yellow color—is thought by some to be a potential solution to the suffering and illness caused by vitamin A deficiency.

J Other experts, however, claim that the biotechnology industry has exaggerated the benefits of golden rice. "Golden rice alone won't greatly **diminish** vitamin A deficiency," says Professor Marion Nestle of New York University. "Beta-carotene,[7] which is already widely available in fruit and vegetables, isn't converted to vitamin A when people are malnourished. Golden rice does not contain much beta-carotene, and whether it will improve vitamin A levels remains to be seen."

Q: What's next?

K Whether biotech foods will deliver on their promise of eliminating world hunger and improving the lives of all remains to be seen. Their potential is enormous, yet they carry risks. If science proceeds with caution, testing new products thoroughly and using sound judgment, the world may avoid the dangers of genetic modification while enjoying its benefits.

be applied to cotton plants that have been genetically modified to produce their own natural pesticides. While applied chemical pesticides kill nearly all the insects in a field, biotech crops with natural pesticides only harm insects that actually try to eat those crops.

Q: Can biotech foods help feed the world?

H "Eight hundred million people on this planet are malnourished,"[6] says Channapatna Prakash, a native of India and a scientist at Tuskegee University's Center for Plant Biotechnology Research in the U.S.A., "and the number continues to grow." Prakash

---

6 Someone who is **malnourished** is weakened from not eating enough food.

7 **Beta-carotene**, a natural substance found in red or orange fruit and vegetables, is used in the body to create vitamin A.

A. Choose the best answer for each question.

PURPOSE
1. What is the author's purpose in writing the passage?

   a. to make biotech foods seem as attractive as possible
   b. to show both sides of the biotech foods issue
   c. to convince the reader that biotech foods are dangerous
   d. to explain why biotech foods will probably not be successful

DETAIL
2. Which of the following is NOT practiced by conventional breeders?

   a. using related organisms to breed
   b. altering the genetic traits of organisms
   c. creating organisms with desired traits
   d. transferring just a few genes at a time from one organism to another

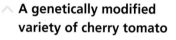

∧ **A genetically modified variety of cherry tomato**

INFERENCE
3. What is the danger of fumonisins?

   a. They might cause cancer in humans.
   b. They could reduce insect resistance in modified corn.
   c. They might cause insects to damage corn plants.
   d. They could kill insects.

DETAIL
4. Which of these concerns about GE crops is NOT mentioned?

   a. Some GE crops are being developed too quickly.
   b. Something could go wrong when moving genes across dramatically different species.
   c. GE crops are being released before they've been adequately tested.
   d. GE species will pollute water and harm animals.

MAIN IDEA
5. What is the main idea of the final paragraph?

   a. With care, the potential of biotech foods could possibly be realized.
   b. The risks of biotech foods seem to outweigh any possible benefits.
   c. The world has already seen great advances due to biotech foods.
   d. Biotech food development has been slowed by the many risks involved.

MATCHING
B. What are some of the effects of genetic alterations on crop production? Match an effect (a–d) with each crop (1–3) according to information from the reading passage. One effect is extra.

1. corn _____   **2.** soybean _____   **3.** cotton _____

   a. It is more nutritious because it contains higher amounts of vitamin C.
   b. It has lower levels of a particular group of toxins.
   c. It requires fewer chemical pesticides, so it is better for the environment.
   d. Since it contains nut proteins, people could have allergic reactions.

Evaluating Arguments

Writers sometimes present two sides of an argument—giving reasons for and against an idea. Understanding both sides is a useful way to consider an issue. It can also help you decide on your own opinion. To evaluate a writer's arguments, it can be useful to list the reasons for and against in a T-chart.

ANALYZING **A.** Look back at Reading B. Find arguments for and against biotech foods in the text.

COMPLETION **B.** Complete the chart below with words or phrases from Reading B.

Arguments for biotech foods	Arguments against biotech foods
Good history People have been changing plants genetically for [1]_____ of years with no problems. **Safe for humans** Studies indicate GE foods do not pose a [2]_____ to human health than non-GE foods. **Environmental benefits** GE crops can produce their own [3]_____ pesticides, so farmers can apply fewer [4]_____ pesticides. **Increased crops** Farmers can grow more crops in areas that are usually not suitable for farming.	**Unexpected consequences** Something could go wrong when genes are moved across different species, with the possibility of [5]_____. **Environmental risks** GE crops are sometimes released into the environment before they have been [6]_____. **Unproven benefits** The health benefits of some GE foods may have been exaggerated.

CRITICAL THINKING Evaluating Arguments

▶ Look at the arguments in the chart above. Underline any evidence from the reading passage (e.g., examples, statistics, expert opinions) that supports each argument.

▶ Based on the information from the reading passage, would you eat genetically modified foods? Why or why not? Note your answers below. Then share with a partner.

_____

_____

COMPLETION **A.** Complete the information using the correct form of words from the box. Two words are extra.

allergic	conventional	diminish
modify	notwithstanding	revolution

According to a recent study, Chinese farmers growing rice that has been genetically ¹_____ successfully reduced pesticide use by 80 percent. The GE rice seed also boosted crop production by almost 10 percent. Some think this could signal a(n) ²_____ in food and agriculture.

However, critics worry that some people may suffer unexpected ³_____ reactions to GE foods. Such fears and concerns ⁴_____, proven examples of problems with GE foods have been quite rare.

⌃ **Genetically modified produce**

WORDS IN CONTEXT **B.** Complete the sentences. Circle the correct words.

1. **Nutritional** food is food that is *bad / good* for you.

2. If you have an **alternative**, there is *a choice / no choice*.

3. A diet **deficient** in protein includes too *much / little* protein.

4. A **conventional** way of doing something is *a new / the usual* way.

5. An example of a plant's **traits** might be its *price / size*.

6. When something **diminishes**, it becomes *smaller / bigger* in size or importance.

WORD USAGE **C.** The words in **bold** below are near synonyms of **diminish**. Circle the correct word to complete each sentence. Use a dictionary or thesaurus to help you.

1. In the United States, crop yields are expected to **fade / decline** because of droughts.

2. Increases in oil production in the United States will **lessen / drop** the need to import oil.

3. Many countries think it's a good idea to **contract / reduce** the amount of pesticides used in agriculture.

4. Some consumers were initially reluctant to buy GE foods—but this resistance has started to **contract / fade**.

Workers check the quality of tomatoes at a food processing plant.

IS OUR FOOD SAFE?

BEFORE YOU WATCH

DISCUSSION

A. Think of the process food goes through from farm to table. At what stages can health risks occur? What are some ways food can make us sick? List some ideas with a partner.

PREVIEWING

B. Read this extract from the video. Match the words and phrases in **bold** with their definitions (1–3).

> "How often does food make us sick? It's **hard to tell** since so many cases go **unreported**. And **globalization** of food production makes it harder and harder to track. But we do know this: At least one in six Americans gets sick from food poisoning every year."

1. _____ : expansion throughout the world
2. _____ : difficult to detect or understand
3. _____ : kept private or hidden

WHILE YOU WATCH

MAIN IDEAS **A.** Watch the video. Check (✓) the ideas that are mentioned.

☐ a. Contaminated water, animals, or equipment can taint food.

☐ b. Symptoms of food poisoning may start within hours after eating contaminated food.

☐ c. The majority of foodborne illnesses in the U.S. is caused by unknown pathogens.

COMPLETION **B.** Watch the video again and complete the notes below.

Annual food poisoning statistics in the U.S.

• number of people who end up hospitalized: 1_____

• number of people killed: 2_____

2011 E. coli outbreak in Germany

• nearly 3_____ people became sick with diarrhea, fever, and vomiting

• officials determined that 4_____ were the real cause

• number of deaths reported: 5_____; number of countries affected: 6_____

CRITICAL THINKING Evaluating Ideas How strongly do you agree with the following statements (1 = strongly disagree; 5 = strongly agree)? Circle your answers. Then discuss with a partner.

1. The government should ban all chemical pesticides. 1 2 3 4 5

2. Restaurants involved in food poisoning cases should face criminal prosecution. 1 2 3 4 5

3. Eating home-cooked meals is safer than dining out. 1 2 3 4 5

VOCABULARY REVIEW

Do you remember the meanings of these words? Check (✓) the ones you know. Look back at the unit and review any words you're not sure of.

Reading A

☐ compulsory ☐ confine* ☐ contaminate ☐ determine ☐ digestion

☐ feasible ☐ infect ☐ integral* ☐ nationwide ☐ optimistic

Reading B

☐ allergic ☐ alternative* ☐ conventional* ☐ deficiency ☐ diminish*

☐ modify* ☐ notwithstanding* ☐ nutritional ☐ revolution* ☐ trait

* Academic Word List

4

DESIGN AND ENGINEERING

The Lotus Temple in Delhi, India, is noted for its half-open lotus flower design.

WARM UP

Discuss these questions with a partner.

1. Think of some famous or innovative buildings. What do you think influenced or inspired their design?

2. Can you think of any man-made objects or machines that were inspired by nature?

4A

DEFINITIONS **A.** Read the information below and match each phrase in **bold** with its definition (1–4).

Biomimetic engineers have a **specific purpose** in mind: to create designs that **have the potential** to change our everyday lives. These engineers **draw inspiration** from designs found in nature, many of which are **incredibly complex**. They then apply the design principles in order to improve existing technologies or to create entirely new ones.

1. _____ : to get ideas
2. _____ : extremely difficult to understand
3. _____ : to possess the capability
4. _____ : a definite goal or aim

SKIMMING **B.** Skim paragraph A and answer these questions.

1. Who is Andrew Parker?
2. What special ability does the thorny devil have?
3. What does Parker want to do with the knowledge he has obtained?

DESIGN BY NATURE:
BIOMIMETICS

A One cloudless midsummer day, biologist Andrew Parker knelt in the baking red sand of an Australian desert and gently placed the right back leg of a thorny devil into a dish of water. The thorny devil—a small lizard that has learned to survive in the extreme heat of the Australian desert—has a secret that fascinated Parker. "Look, look!" he exclaimed. "Its back is completely drenched!"[1] Sure enough, in less than a minute, water from the dish had traveled up the lizard's leg, across its skin, and into its mouth. It was, in essence, drinking through its foot. The thorny devil can also do this when standing on wet sand—a **vital** competitive advantage in the desert. Parker had come here to solve the riddle of how it does this, not from purely **biological** interest, but with a specific purpose in mind: to make a **device** to help people collect water in the desert.

From Natural Wonder to Useful Tool

B Parker is a leading scientist in the field of biomimetics—applying designs from nature to solve problems in engineering, materials science, medicine, and other fields. His studies of the body coverings of butterflies and beetles have led to brighter screens for cell phones. He has even drawn inspiration from nature's past: While visiting a museum in Poland, he noticed a 45-million-year-old fly trapped in amber[2] and observed how the shape of its eye's surface reduced light reflection. This shape is now being used in solar panels to make them more efficient.

---

1 If something is **drenched**, it is completely wet.
2 **Amber** is a hard yellowish-brown substance used for making jewelry.

‹ **A thorny devil lizard**

Cockleburs have hooked spines that attach to clothing and animal fur. This design inspired the creation of Velcro (right).

C   As part of the next **phase** in his plan to create a water-collection device inspired by the lizard, Parker sent his observations to Michael Rubner and Robert Cohen, two colleagues at the Massachusetts Institute of Technology. Parker is full of enthusiasm about the many possibilities of biomimetics. Rubner and Cohen, on the other hand, are much more practical; they focus on the ideas that have a chance of being applied successfully. This combination of biological **insight** and engineering pragmatism[3] is vital to success in biomimetics. And it has led to several promising technologies.

D   Though Rubner and Cohen are certainly impressed by biological structures, they consider nature just a starting point for innovation. Cohen says, "The natural structure provides a clue to what is useful … But maybe you can do it better." They consider a biomimetics project a success only if it has the potential to make a useful tool for people. "Looking at pretty structures in nature is not sufficient," says Cohen. "What I want to know is can we actually transform these structures into [something] with true utility[4] in the real world?"

Unlocking Nature's Secrets

E   The work of Parker, Rubner, and Cohen is only one part of a growing global biomimetics movement. Scientists around the world are studying and trying to copy a wide variety of nature's design secrets. In the United States, researchers are looking at the shape of humpback whale fins in order to help wind turbines

---

3 **Pragmatism** means dealing with problems in a practical way.

4 The **utility** of something is its usefulness.

A close-up
look at Velcro

generate more electric energy. The shape of the body of a certain fish has inspired designers at Mercedes-Benz to develop a more efficient car design. By analyzing how termites[5] keep their large mounds at the right temperature and humidity, architects in Zimbabwe have built more comfortable buildings. And in Japan, medical researchers have developed a painless needle that is similar in shape to the proboscis[6] of a mosquito.

The Bio-Inspired Robot

F Potentially, one of the most useful applications of biomimetics is the robot. Robots can perform tasks that might be too boring or dangerous for humans, but they can be extremely difficult to build. Professor Ronald Fearing of the University of California is creating a tiny robot fly that can be used in surveillance[7] or rescue operations. Fearing's fly is a simplified copy of the real thing. "Some things are just too mysterious and complicated to be able to replicate,"[8] he says. It will still be years before his robot fly can perform anything like an actual fly, but Fearing is confident that over time he will close the **gap** between nature and human engineering.

G At Stanford University in California, Mark Cutkosky is working on a robot gecko. Cutkosky studied the extremely small structures on the tiny lizard's feet that allow it to run up and down **vertical** walls. He applied what he learned to create

---

5 **Termites** are small insects that eat wood.

6 A **proboscis** is a long mouth part, usually of an insect.

7 **Surveillance** is the close observation of a person or place, especially by the police or army.

8 If you **replicate** something, you make a copy of it.

Stickybot, a robot that can walk up and down smooth vertical surfaces. The U.S. military, which **funds** the project, hopes that one day Stickybot will be able to climb up a building and stay there for days, monitoring the area below. Cutkosky believes there will be a range of nonmilitary uses as well. "I'm trying to get robots to go places where they've never gone before," he says. For now, Stickybot can only climb extremely smooth surfaces—unlike a real gecko, which can run up just about any surface very quickly.

H Despite the promise of the field and the brilliant people who work in it, biomimetics has led to surprisingly few business successes. Perhaps only one product has become truly famous—Velcro. The material was invented in 1948 by Swiss engineer George de Mestral, who copied the way seeds called cockleburs stuck to his dog's fur. Some blame industry, whose short-term expectations about how soon a project should be completed and become profitable conflict with the time-consuming nature of biomimetics research. But the main reason biomimetics hasn't yet been a business success is that nature is incredibly complex.

I **Nonetheless**, the gap with nature is **gradually** closing. Researchers are using more powerful microscopes, high-speed computers, and other new technologies to learn more from nature. A growing number of biomimetic materials are being produced. And although the field of biomimetics has yet to become a very successful commercial industry, it has already developed into a powerful tool for understanding nature's secrets.

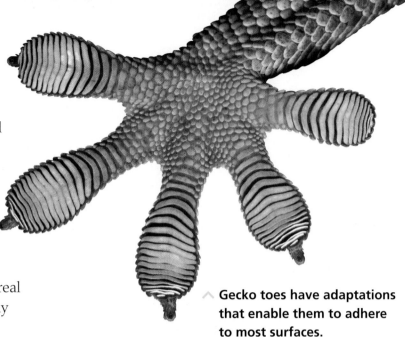

∧ Gecko toes have adaptations that enable them to adhere to most surfaces.

MORE NATURE-INSPIRED INNOVATIONS

- A type of glass has been created that draws inspiration from spider webs. Birds can see the ultraviolet reflective strands in the glass, and thus avoid flying into it.

- Water does not stick to a lotus leaf because of its surface structure. Copying this process, one company has developed a water-repelling sealant that can be sprayed on surfaces.

- Swimmers can now swim faster because of new suits that mimic the design of sharkskin. This design is also used to reduce friction on ships, submarines, and airplanes.

- High-speed trains have long beak-shaped noses, modeled after the kingfisher bird. This reduces noise and allows the train to travel much faster.

- A new fan on the market is based on the spiral shape seen in tornadoes and whirlpools. The fan cools the air more efficiently than traditional fans.

∧ A swimmer tests a new swimsuit designed to increase speed.

A. Choose the best answer for each question.

DETAIL

1. Why did Andrew Parker go to the Australian desert?

    a. to capture and bring back a thorny devil
    b. to learn how the thorny devil collects water
    c. to study the diet of the thorny devil
    d. to prove that thorny devils don't need water

DETAIL

2. What has the study of termite mounds inspired?

    a. a more efficient car design
    b. improved wind turbines
    c. more comfortable buildings
    d. a painless needle

REFERENCE

3. What does *things* in Ronald Fearing's quote "Some things are just too mysterious and complicated …" (paragraph F) refer to?

    a. abilities
    b. robot flies
    c. copies
    d. rescue operations

DETAIL

4. According to the passage, what is a limitation of Stickybot?

    a. It can't climb up rough, uneven surfaces.
    b. It can move forward but not backward.
    c. It is too heavy to stay on a wall for long.
    d. The military won't let others use the technology.

DETAIL

5. Which of these statements about biomimetics is NOT true?

    a. Parker hopes to create a water-collection device inspired by the thorny devil.
    b. Studying humpback whale fins may be useful for improving wind turbines.
    c. The body of a certain fish has inspired a car design.
    d. Stickybot is perhaps the most famous biomimetic creation so far.

MATCHING

B. What are some applications of biomimetics? Match each application (1–4) with the animal trait that inspired it (a–d).

    a. butterfly body coverings
    b. spider webs
    c. sharkskin
    d. kingfisher beaks

    _____ **1.** make rail travel quieter and faster
    _____ **2.** develop brighter cell phone screens
    _____ **3.** create a type of glass that is more bird-friendly
    _____ **4.** design new swimwear that can make swimmers move faster

> **The kingfisher has a long, narrow beak.**

Scanning for Information (2)—Matching Information to Paragraphs

Scanning is an important skill for taking exams, but how you approach scanning should depend on the question type. With **matching information questions**, you have to match statements about reasons, descriptions, examples, and so forth from a text to particular paragraphs. First, read each statement carefully and identify key words or phrases. These exact words may not appear in the passage, so you will need to think of synonyms or antonyms that might. For example, if you are asked to find a prediction, you might want to scan for "will" in the text.

MATCHING **A.** Read the sentences below (1–3) from Reading A. Match each sentence with the type of information it contains (a–c).

1. Cutkosky believes there will be a range of nonmilitary uses as well.   •   • a. a reason

2. For now, Stickybot can only climb extremely smooth surfaces—unlike a real gecko, which can run up just about any surface very quickly.   •   • b. a prediction

3. The main reason biomimetics hasn't yet been a business success is that nature is incredibly complex.   •   • c. a contrast

SCANNING **B.** Find the following information in Reading A and note which paragraph (A–I) each item appears in.

_____ 1. a definition of biomimetics

_____ 2. a prediction about the future of robot flies

_____ 3. the reason the U.S. military is financing a biomimetic project

_____ 4. an example of a biomimetic product that has become truly famous

CRITICAL THINKING Applying Ideas   Work in a group. Imagine you are tasked with inventing a new biomimetic application. Look at the animal attributes below. Choose one and come up with a biomimetic application for it.

- worms that glow in the dark
- snakes that shed their skin
- beavers that have waterproof fur
- octopuses that can change color

< **A bioluminescent European glow-worm**

VOCABULARY PRACTICE

COMPLETION **A.** Circle the correct words to complete the paragraph.

One of the earliest examples of biomimicry is the Eastgate Centre in Harare, Zimbabwe. Designed by the architect Mick Pearce, this large office building doesn't use conventional heating or air conditioning, but is ¹**nonetheless / vital** regulated such that it is never too hot or too cold. Pearce noticed that African termites keep their mounds cool inside by using a clever system of air vents that open and close, regulating temperature. This ²**phase / insight** inspired him to design the Eastgate Centre to work in a similar way. A series of ³**funds / gaps**, vents, and ⁴**vertical / gradual** chimneys move air through the building—using less than 10 percent of the energy of a conventional building its size. As the temperature ⁵**gradually / biologically** rises and falls outside, it stays comfortable inside.

∧ **Eastgate Centre, Harare, Zimbabwe**

WORDS IN CONTEXT **B.** Complete each sentence with the correct answer (a or b).

1. If an organization **funds** a project, they _____ it.

   a. are inspired by   b. pay for

2. **Biological** processes are those that describe _____ .

   a. living organisms   b. mechanical objects

3. A **device** is an object created _____ .

   a. by natural processes   b. for a particular purpose

4. A **phase** of an engineering project refers to _____ .

   a. its overall cost   b. a particular stage

5. Something that is **vital** is _____ .

   a. necessary   b. disproved by others

COLLOCATIONS **C.** The words in the box are often used with the word **vital**. Complete the sentences with the correct words from the box. One word is extra.

absolutely	importance	link	role

1. The tourism industry is of vital _____ to the national economy.

2. Biomimetic research is _____ vital if we wish to develop more sustainable solutions to human challenges in design and engineering.

3. Mick Pearce has played a vital _____ in designing eco-friendly buildings in Africa.

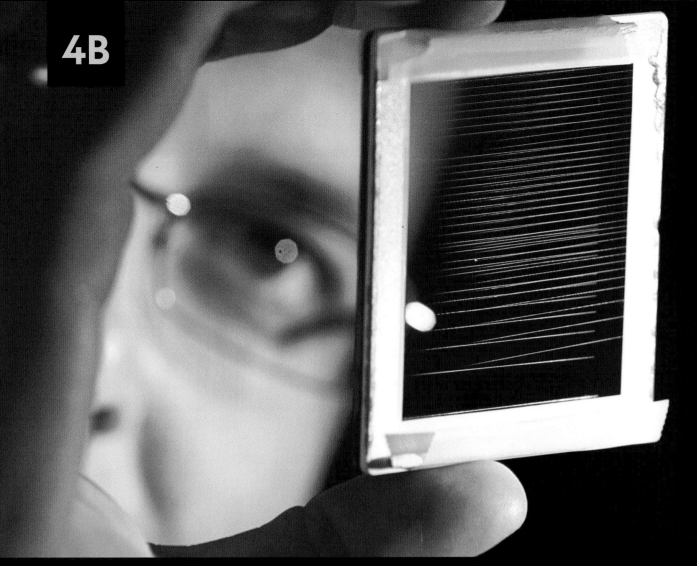

∧ Biochemist Thomas Scheibel holds a frame containing **synthetic** spider's thread. This artificial **fiber**—stronger than real silk—could be used to create **textiles** for clothing and other products.

BEFORE YOU READ

DEFINITIONS **A.** Read the caption above. Use the words in **bold** to complete these definitions (1–3).

    1. _____ are types of woven cloth.

    2. A _____ is a thin thread of a natural or artificial substance.

    3. _____ products are made from chemicals or artificial substances.

PREDICTING **B.** What are some recent innovations in textiles and clothing? Discuss with a partner and note some ideas. Then read the passage and check if any of your ideas are mentioned.

_____

_____

WEAVING THE FUTURE

A Alex Soza is a young Danish fashion designer. He says his ideas come to him in dreams: "I daydream. That's how I get ideas." One of his inventions, a jacket that stays **suspended** in the air like a balloon after it is taken off, arose from such a daydream. "I was on the subway," he explained, "and this picture of a floating jacket popped into my mind." Soza is one of many dreamers and pioneers who are turning textile **fantasies** into realities.

High-Tech Textiles

B Not long ago, all fibers that were used to make textiles came from natural sources: wool from the hair of sheep, cotton from the cotton plant, silk from silk worms. The first truly synthetic fiber didn't appear until 1935, when scientists at the DuPont Company invented nylon. Nylon is just one of various industrially produced substances called polymers. Polymers can be pulled into a thread, which makes them well suited for use in textile **manufacturing**.

C Synthetic textiles have come a long way since nylon. Kevlar, a textile that is stronger than steel, is used in bulletproof vests and in ropes used by astronauts. Coiled fibers are used in clothing that contracts in cold weather to keep someone warm, and expands in hot weather, creating small holes to keep someone cool. Other high-tech fibers can resist very high temperatures—perfect for firefighters and race-car drivers.

D Not all companies are **forthcoming** about their products for fear of having their ideas stolen. However, Hugues Vinchon, a manager at Dubar Warneton—a manufacturer of high-tech textiles in France—is happy to display some of his company's amazing synthetic fibers. There is an oil-eating textile that absorbs five times its weight in oil, and is perfect for cleaning up oil spills. Another absorbs vibrations;[1] "Can you imagine a motorboat you

---

1 A **vibration** is a small, fast, and continuous shaking movement.

Sensors on this smart shirt can monitor the wearer's breathing and transmit the data to a cell phone.

can't hear?" he says. There is also an ordinary-looking cloth bag that is completely water soluble,[2] according to Vinchon. "It's strong enough to carry heavy objects. But if I dip it in boiling water, it disappears."

E Some high-tech textiles draw their inspiration from nature. Spider silk is a natural fiber that is five times as strong as steel. Unfortunately, spiders cannot be farmed as they will eat each other. The biotechnology firm Nexia has come up with a possible alternative to spider farming: They have inserted a spider gene into goats, **thereby** causing the goats to produce a milk that contains a protein required for spider silk. Nexia's head, Jeff Turner, is already dreaming of applications for the new fiber, named BioSteel. "Why use rockets to lift objects into orbit?[3] … Why not have a [big] satellite and dangle a rope down to Earth and pull them up? … [There's] not a rope that will hold its weight at that length—but spider silk with its high strength-to-weight ratio could."

Wearable Electronics

F Textiles have always been used in clothing. Modern, high-tech textiles may redefine what clothes are all about. "In the past, clothing protected us from the elements," says Ian Scott, head of technology for women's wear at department store Marks & Spencer. "Then clothing became about fashion. The future is about clothing that can do something for you. It's no longer passive. It's active." One example of this active clothing that he hopes to sell in the next few years is an "intelligent bra," a sports bra that can sense stress and adjust its dimensions to give perfect support. Another sports product is Komodo Technologies' smart sleeve for athletes. It has built-in sensors[4] that measure your fitness

---

2 If something is water **soluble**, it will dissolve in water.
3 An **orbit** is the curved path in space that an object follows as it moves around a planet, moon, or star.
4 A **sensor** is an instrument that reacts to certain physical conditions, such as heat or light.

and stress levels. The data can then be viewed on a smartphone app. The company is also researching ways the sleeve can help detect heart disease.

G Other wearable electronics are being pioneered at a design laboratory in London run by the European manufacturer Philips Electronics. They are in the planning stages for various high-tech products, including an "intelligent" electronic apron. This smart apron acts as a kind of remote-control device. It has a built-in microphone that allows the wearer to operate kitchen **appliances** using voice commands.

H While there are many interesting clothing innovations in the pipeline, few have hit the market. One that did was marketed a few years ago as the first wearable electronics jacket. The jacket, called the ICD+, sold for about a thousand dollars. It had an MP3 player and cell phone. Headphones were built into the hood, and it had a microphone in the collar. Clive

van Heerden, director of the Intelligent Fibres group of Philips Design, pointed out that it was an early first step, and a conservative one: "We want to make the jacket that makes the coffee and picks up the kids and keeps track of the shopping list, but it's not going to happen overnight."

Future Warriors

I One of the most important areas of clothing innovation is for the military. High-tech textiles are everywhere at the U.S. Army Soldier Systems Center in Natick, Massachusetts. As part of their Future Warrior program, researchers are developing uniforms that will make a soldier difficult or impossible to see. Fibers in the uniform would take on the same color, brightness, and patterns of the wearer's surroundings. A soldier dressed in such a uniform would become nearly invisible to the enemy.

J In addition to clothing innovations, the researchers at Natick are also working on **portable** buildings made of what are essentially large, high-strength textile balloons. This "airbeam" technology would allow a team to build a hangar[5] in a **fraction** of the time it would take to build one out of metal. The largest air-filled beams, about 0.75 meters in diameter and 24 meters long, are so **rigid** that you can hang a heavy truck from one. Whereas a conventional metal hangar takes ten people five days to set up, one made of airbeams can be set up by just six people in two days.

K Today's textile innovations are astonishing. From Alex Soza's artistic jacket to smart aprons to invisible military uniforms, high-tech textiles will soon be appearing in more and more places. Who can **foresee** what these textile innovators will dream up next? "It's about imagination!" says Soza, with a bright look in his eye. "It's a beautiful dream! It's turning science fiction into scientific fact!"

---

5 A **hangar** is a large building in which aircraft are kept.

A. Choose the best answer for each question.

PURPOSE

1. What is the main purpose of the passage?

a. to provide a historical overview of innovative fashion styles
b. to introduce the reader to developments in high-tech textiles
c. to convince the reader to buy the latest synthetic fashions
d. to explain how modern fashions are often inspired by nature

INFERENCE

2. Why does Hugues Vinchon mention a motorboat you can't hear?

a. to explain one of the properties of an oil-absorbing fabric
b. to give an example of how quietly his textile factory runs
c. to evoke admiration for a fabric that can absorb vibrations
d. to show that he is not afraid of having his ideas stolen

INFERENCE

3. Which person do you think would be most likely to design a coat made of paper with six sleeves that three people can wear together?

a. Alex Soza
b. Hugues Vinchon
c. Jeff Turner
d. Ian Scott

PARAPHRASE

4. What does Clive van Heerden mean, when talking about the jacket, that "it's not going to happen overnight" (paragraph H)?

a. It's not going to happen until tomorrow.
b. It's going to take a short time to happen.
c. It's going to take a long time to happen.
d. It's probably never going to happen.

COHESION

5. The following sentence would best be placed at the end of which paragraph?
Thanks to them, the world of high-tech textiles is an exciting place to be these days.

a. paragraph A
b. paragraph B
c. paragraph I
d. paragraph K

SCANNING

Review this reading skill in Unit 4A

B. Find the following information in the passage. Note which paragraph (A–K) each item appears in.

_____ **1.** a reason why there are no spider farms

_____ **2.** three examples of fibers from natural sources

_____ **3.** a quote from someone who discusses science fiction

_____ **4.** the purpose of everyday clothing in the past

_____ **5.** an explanation of how a fashion designer gets his ideas

Recognizing Lexical Cohesion

Writers use different techniques to avoid repetition in order to add interest and variety to a text. Recognizing how a writer achieves lexical cohesion allows you to better understand the flow of ideas and the relationship between them. Look at some of the following ways a writer can achieve lexical cohesion:

Synonyms: Using a word that means the same (or nearly the same) as another word (e.g., *cold, icy*).

Antonyms: Using a word that means the opposite of another word (e.g., *big, small*).

Repetition: Repeating the same word, or using a different form of the word (e.g., *manufactures, manufacturing*).

Reference: Using a pronoun or determiner that refers back to another word (e.g., *fibers, they*).

Subordination: Using a specific example of a more general word (e.g., *fibers, silk*).

RECOGNIZING
LEXICAL COHESION

A. Read the sentences below from Reading B. Note if the two underlined words in each item are examples of **A** (antonyms), **RP** (repetition), **RF** (reference), or **SU** (subordination).

1. Not long ago, all fibers that were used to make textiles came from <u>natural</u> sources … The first truly <u>synthetic</u> fiber didn't appear until 1935. _____

2. <u>Nylon</u> is just one of various industrially produced substances called <u>polymers</u>. _____

3. <u>Polymers</u> can be pulled into a thread, which makes <u>them</u> well suited for use in textile manufacturing. _____

4. Coiled fibers are used in clothing that contracts in cold weather to keep someone <u>warm</u>, and expands in hot weather, creating small holes to keep someone <u>cool</u>. _____

5. Textiles have always been used in <u>clothing</u>. Modern, high-tech textiles may redefine what <u>clothes</u> are all about. _____

RECOGNIZING
LEXICAL COHESION

B. Look back at Reading B to find these examples of lexical cohesion.

1. an antonym of *passive* in paragraph F _____

2. a synonym of *intelligent* in paragraph G _____

3. the word(s) referred to by *It* in paragraph G, line 7 _____

4. a synonym of *impossible to see* in paragraph I _____

5. a different form of the word *innovations* in paragraph K _____

CRITICAL THINKING Applying Ideas   Can you think of possible future applications of wearable electronics? Discuss with a partner and note your ideas below.

_____

_____

VOCABULARY PRACTICE

COMPLETION   **A.** Complete the paragraph with words from the box.

fantasy	rigid	suspended	thereby

The Mastaba, London

The artist Christo uses colorful man-made materials to temporarily change how an outdoor place looks, ¹_____ allowing people to see the place in a new way. In *The Gates*, large sheets of orange fabric were ²_____ over 7,500 vinyl frames and placed around Central Park in New York. In *The Mastaba*, Christo used over 7,000 oil barrels painted pink and blue to construct a large, ³_____ sculpture that floated on a lake in London. It takes an incredible amount of time to construct these kinds of projects. Once Christo settles on an artistic idea, it takes time, work, and money to turn his ⁴_____ into reality.

DEFINITIONS   **B.** Match the words in the box with the definitions below.

appliance	foresee	forthcoming
fraction	manufacturing	portable

1. _____ : able to be easily carried or moved
2. _____ : a small part or amount of something
3. _____ : a device (often electrical) used at home
4. _____ : to realize something before it happens
5. _____ : willing to give information or to talk
6. _____ : the business of producing goods on a large scale

WORD PARTS   **C.** The prefix *fore-* in **foresee** means "before." Complete the sentences using the words in the box. One word is extra.

cast	front	ground	sight

1. Sales of smart clothing are **fore**_____ to rise in the future.
2. Steve Jobs had the **fore**_____ to reimagine the cell phone.
3. Companies like Philips Electronics are at the **fore**_____ of wearable technologies.

ROBOTIC HANDS

> A new kind of robot is tested in the deep waters of the Red Sea.

BEFORE YOU WATCH

PREVIEWING **A.** Read the information. The words in **bold** appear in the video. Match these words with their definitions below.

Marine biologists collect samples of deep-sea **corals** in order to analyze their **genomes** and other characteristics. They often use underwater robots to collect samples from the ocean. Unfortunately, these mechanical "hands" can destroy **fragile** marine life—their hard, metal fingers are unable to **grab** deep-sea organisms without damaging them. Marine biologist David Gruber and roboticist Robert Wood are now developing a new kind of robot to address this problem.

1. coral •   • a. easily broken or damaged

2. genome •   • b. to hold tightly

3. fragile •   • c. the complete set of genetic information in an organism

4. grab •   • d. a hard substance formed in the sea from the bones of very small sea animals

DISCUSSION **B.** Look at the photo above and read the caption. How might this robotic hand be better suited for collecting deep-sea organisms? Discuss with a partner.

GIST **A.** Watch the video. Check (✓) two things that are shown in the video.

☐ a. the development of the squishy robot fingers in a lab

☐ b. scientists testing the squishy robot fingers in a deep-sea environment

☐ c. above-water applications of the squishy robot fingers

EVALUATING STATEMENTS **B.** Watch the video again. Are the following statements true or false? Circle **T** (true) or **F** (false).

1. The team is testing the squishy robot fingers in the Red Sea because it is a very rich coral environment.	T	F
2. The squishy robot fingers are made of rubber.	T	F
3. The squishy robot fingers were originally developed for oil exploration.	T	F
4. The squishy robot fingers do not work well on land.	T	F
5. The deep-sea test of the squishy robot fingers was successful.	T	F

CRITICAL THINKING Applying Ideas | Work in a small group and discuss these questions.

▶ Which trait or ability of an animal or a plant not mentioned in this unit do you think would be useful to replicate? Brainstorm a list of attributes and note your ideas below.

_____

_____

▶ Choose one of your ideas above. Can you think of a practical use for it?

_____

VOCABULARY REVIEW

Do you remember the meanings of these words? Check (✓) the ones you know. Look back at the unit and review any words you're not sure of.

Reading A

☐ biological   ☐ device*   ☐ fund*   ☐ gap   ☐ gradually

☐ insight*   ☐ nonetheless   ☐ phase*   ☐ vertical   ☐ vital

Reading B

☐ appliance   ☐ fantasy   ☐ foresee   ☐ forthcoming*   ☐ fraction

☐ manufacturing   ☐ portable   ☐ rigid*   ☐ suspend*   ☐ thereby

* Academic Word List

5

HUMAN JOURNEY

⌄ A reenactment of the migration of early human hunter-gatherers

Discuss these questions with a partner.

1. What do you know about the lives of early humans?

2. What kinds of evidence help us learn about our human ancestors?

79

BEFORE YOU READ

UNDERSTANDING MAPS

A. The map on page 82 shows the likely migration routes of our human ancestors as they populated the world. Study the map and complete each of these sentences with the name of a continent.

1. The first modern humans originally came from _____ .

2. The continent most recently populated by modern humans is _____ .

3. Modern humans crossed over to North America from _____ .

4. _____ was populated by modern humans 40,000–30,000 years ago.

SKIMMING

B. Skim the reading passage on the next three pages. What kinds of evidence are scientists looking for to understand the migrations of our human ancestors?

> As our human ancestors spread out across the continents, they gave rise to a variety of faces and races.

THE DNA TRAIL

A   Everybody loves a good story, and when it's finished, this may be the greatest one ever told. It begins in Africa with a group of people. There are perhaps just a few hundred, surviving by hunting animals and gathering fruits, vegetables, and nuts. It ends about 200,000 years later, with their seven billion **descendants** spread across the Earth.

B   In between is an exciting tale of survival, movement, isolation, and conquest, most of it occurring before recorded history. Who were those first modern people in Africa? What routes did they take when they left their home continent to expand into Europe and Asia? When and how did humans reach the Americas? For decades, the only proof was found in a small number of **scattered** bones and artifacts that our ancestors had left behind. In the past 20 years, however, DNA technologies have allowed scientists to find a record of ancient human migrations in the DNA of living people.

Tracing Ancestry in DNA

C   "Every drop of human blood contains a history book written in the language of our genes," says population geneticist[1] Spencer Wells. The human genetic code, or genome, is 99.9 percent **identical** throughout the world. The **bulk** of our DNA is the same. However, the remainder is responsible for our individual differences—in eye color or disease risk, for example. On very rare occasions, a small change—called a mutation—can occur. This can then be passed down to all of that person's descendants. Generations later, finding that same mutation in two people's DNA indicates that they share the same ancestor. By comparing mutations in many different populations, scientists can **trace** their ancestral connections.

D   These ancient mutations are easiest to track in two places. One is in DNA that is passed from mother to child (called mitochondrial DNA, or mtDNA). The other is in DNA that travels from father to son (known as the Y chromosome, the part of DNA that determines a child will be a boy). By comparing the mtDNA and Y chromosomes of people from various populations, geneticists can get a rough idea of where and when those groups separated in the great migrations around the planet.

---

1 A **geneticist** is a scientist who studies DNA and genes.

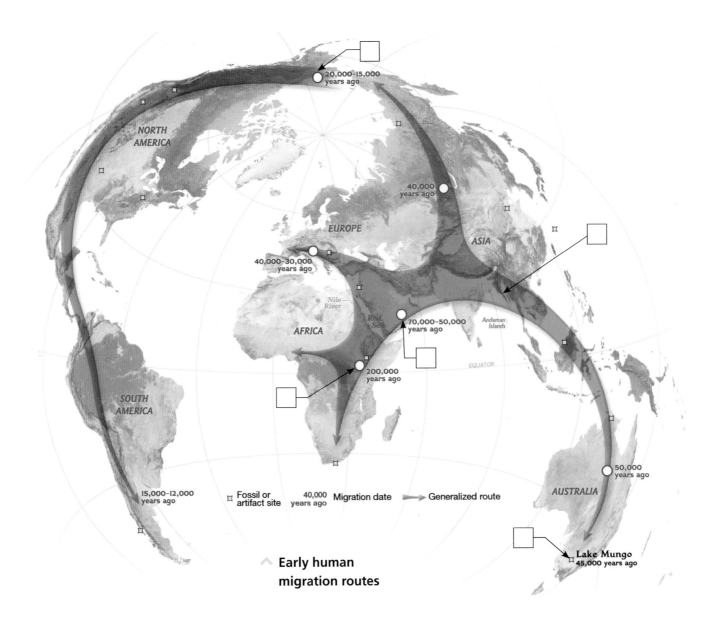

20,000–15,000 years ago

NORTH AMERICA

40,000 years ago

EUROPE

ASIA

40,000–30,000 years ago

Nile River

Red Sea

AFRICA

70,000–50,000 years ago

Andaman Islands

EQUATOR

200,000 years ago

SOUTH AMERICA

15,000–12,000 years ago

⊠ Fossil or artifact site

40,000 years ago Migration date

Generalized route

50,000 years ago

AUSTRALIA

Lake Mungo 45,000 years ago

⋀ **Early human migration routes**

Out of Africa

E   In the mid-1980s, a study compared mtDNA from people around the world. It found that people of African descent had twice as many genetic differences from each other than did others. Because mutations seem to occur at a steady **rate** over time, scientists concluded that modern humans must have lived in Africa at least twice as long as anywhere else. They now **calculate** that all living humans maternally descend from a single woman who lived **roughly** 150,000 years ago in Africa, a "mitochondrial Eve." If geneticists are right, all of humanity is linked to Eve through an unbroken chain of mothers. This Eve was soon joined by "Y-chromosome Adam," the possible genetic father of us all, also from Africa. DNA studies have confirmed that all the people on Earth can trace their ancestry to ancient Africans.

F   What seems certain is that at a remarkably recent date—probably between 50,000 and 70,000 years ago—one small group of people, the ancestors of modern humans outside of Africa, left Africa for western Asia. They either migrated around the wider northern end of the Red Sea, or across its narrow southern opening.

G   Once in Asia, genetic evidence suggests, the population split. One group stayed temporarily in the Middle East, while the other began a journey that would last tens of thousands of years. Moving a little farther with each new generation, they followed the coast around the Arabian Peninsula, India, and Southeast Asia, all the way to Australia. "The movement was probably imperceptible," says Spencer Wells. "It was less of a journey and probably more like walking a little farther down the beach to get away from the crowd."

H   Archeological evidence of this 13,000-kilometer migration from Africa to Australia has almost completely **vanished**. However, genetic traces of the group that made the trip do exist. They have been found in the DNA of indigenous[2] peoples in Malaysia, in Papua New Guinea, and in the DNA of nearly all Australian aborigines. Modern discoveries of 45,000-year-old bodies in Australia, buried at a site called Lake Mungo, provide physical evidence for the theories as well.

I   People in the rest of Asia and Europe share different but equally ancient mtDNA and Y-chromosome mutations. These mutations show that most are descendants of the group that stayed in the Middle East for thousands of years before moving on. Perhaps about 40,000 years ago, modern humans first advanced into Europe.

Peopling the Americas

J   About the same time as modern humans pushed into Europe, some of the same group that had paused in the Middle East spread east into Central Asia. They eventually reached as far as Siberia, the Korean peninsula, and Japan. Here begins one of the last chapters in the human story— the peopling of the Americas. Most scientists believe that today's Native Americans descend from ancient Asians who crossed from Siberia to Alaska in the last ice age. At that time, low sea levels would have exposed a land bridge between the continents. Perhaps they—only a few hundred people—were traveling along the coast, moving from one piece of land to the next, between a freezing ocean and a wall of ice. "A coastal route would have been the easiest way in," says Wells. "But it still would have been a hell of a trip." Once across, they followed the **immense** herds[3] of animals into the mainland. They spread to the tip of South America in as little as a thousand years.

ALTERNATIVE ROUTES?

Scientists have long believed that modern humans originated in Africa, because that's where they've found the oldest bones. Geneticists have come to the same conclusion based on analysis of human DNA. However, there is less consensus about the routes our ancestors took. For example, genetic data suggests that Europe might have been settled by an inland migration from India, rather than directly from the Middle East. "I think the broad human prehistoric framework is in place," says geneticist Peter Forster of the McDonald Institute for Archaeological Research, "and we are now fitting in the details."

K   Genetic researchers can only tell us the basic outlines of a story of human migration that is more complex than any ever written. Many details of the movements of our ancestors and their countless individual lives can only be imagined. But thanks to genetic researchers—themselves descendants of mtDNA Eve and Y-chromosome Adam—we have begun to unlock important secrets about the origins and movements of our ancient ancestors.

---

2 **Indigenous** people or things belong to the country in which they are found, rather than coming there or being brought there from another country.

3 A **herd** is a large group of animals of the same type that live together.

A. Choose the best answer for each question.

GIST

1. What could be another title for this reading?

    a. Finding Y-Chromosome Adam   c. What DNA Teaches Us about Our Past

    b. Who Were the First Humans?   d. The Discovery of DNA in Africa

PARAPHRASE

2. Which of the following is closest in meaning to "Every drop of human blood contains a history book written in the language of our genes" (paragraph C)?

    a. A drop of blood contains information that can reveal a person's ancestral history.

    b. The organization of information in a history book is similar to the structure of DNA.

    c. Every drop of blood contains enough DNA information to fill many history books.

    d. Although people speak different languages, all human blood is similar.

DETAIL

3. What is true about the first group of humans that moved from Africa into Asia?

    a. Most of the migrants turned back into Africa.

    b. They divided into two groups.

    c. Most of the migrants moved quickly into Europe.

    d. They all stayed in the Middle East for thousands of years.

VOCABULARY

4. In paragraph G, the word *imperceptible* could be replaced with _____.

    a. unnoticeable   c. unpredictable

    b. illogical   d. unbelievable

FACT OR THEORY

5. Which statement is a theory, not a fact according to the passage?

    a. Mutations are easiest to find in mtDNA and in the Y chromosome.

    b. The majority of DNA is the same for humans across the world.

    c. The bodies found at Lake Mungo are tens of thousands of years old.

    d. Humans traveled along the coast of a land bridge between Siberia and Alaska.

RECOGNIZING LEXICAL COHESION

Review this reading skill in Unit 4B

B. These sentences from the passage (1–5) contain examples of lexical cohesion. Match each pair of underlined words with the type of lexical cohesion (a–e).

| a. synonym   b. antonym   c. repetition   d. reference   e. subordination |

1. In between is an exciting <u>tale</u> of survival, movement, isolation, and conquest, most of <u>it</u> occurring before recorded history. ____

2. … people of African <u>descent</u> had twice as many genetic differences … . … all living humans maternally <u>descend</u> from a single woman … ____

3. They now calculate that all living <u>humans</u> maternally descend from a single <u>woman</u> who lived roughly 150,000 years ago in Africa … ____

4. They either migrated around the <u>wider</u> northern end of the Red Sea, or across its <u>narrow</u> southern opening. ____

5. Perhaps they … were <u>traveling</u> along the coast, <u>moving</u> from one piece of land to the next. ____

Synthesizing Information

Many reading passages contain visuals such as photos and maps that illustrate information from the passage; the ideas in the passage may also be supported by photo captions and sidebars. Synthesizing—connecting—information from the text with these other features will help you more fully comprehend the passage.

SYNTHESIZING **A.** Read these paraphrased sentences from Reading A. Then label the parts of the map on page 82 that are being referenced (1–5).

    1. Scientists have concluded that all living humans maternally descend from a single woman who lived a long time ago in Africa.

    2. Probably between 50,000 and 70,000 years ago, one small group of people left Africa for western Asia.

    3. Moving a little farther with each new generation, they followed the coast toward Southeast Asia.

    4. Modern discoveries of 45,000-year-old bodies in Australia, buried at a site called Lake Mungo, provide physical evidence for the theories.

    5. Most scientists believe that today's Native Americans descend from ancient Asians who crossed from Siberia to Alaska during the last ice age.

SYNTHESIZING **B.** Read the sidebar "Alternative Routes?" on page 83 and answer the questions below with a partner.

    1. How does the information about Europe expand on the reading passage?

    2. Peter Forster says, "I think the broad human prehistoric framework is in place." Which idea in paragraph K does this expert opinion support?

    3. What is one discovery from the reading passage that has helped "fit in the details"?

CRITICAL THINKING Reflecting/Evaluating   Discuss these questions with a partner.

▶ Humans continue to migrate around the world today. What are some possible reasons for the current migrations? Note your ideas below.

_____

_____

▶ What are the implications of current human migration? Consider both positive and negative effects.

Positive effects: _____

Negative effects: _____

COMPLETION **A.** Complete the paragraph with words from the box. Four words are extra.

bulk	calculate	descendant	identical	immense
rate	roughly	scattered	trace	vanished

A sculpture of a Neanderthal draws attention from passersby in Dusseldorf, Germany.

Before modern humans, or *Homo sapiens*, migrated out of Africa, Neanderthals had occupied parts of Europe and Asia for [1]_____ 200,000 years. Scientists [2]_____ that there were no more than 15,000 of them at their population's peak. They were, however, [3]_____ over a(n) [4]_____ area throughout Europe, the Middle East, and Asia. They were shorter than modern humans, but stronger. Their tools were rough and simple. Additionally, their food was not as varied; the [5]_____ of their diet was meat. At some point, the Neanderthals [6]_____ from Earth. The reason remains a mystery. Modern *Homo sapiens* may have killed them off, or they may have died from disease or climate change.

DEFINITIONS **B.** Match the words in **red** in activity A with these definitions (1–5).

1. _____ : the main or largest part of something

2. _____ : similar in every detail; exactly alike

3. _____ : to follow something to its origin

4. _____ : a person related to someone from an earlier generation

5. _____ : the speed at which something happens, or the number of times it happens in a particular period

COLLOCATIONS **C.** The words in the box are often used with the word **rate**. Complete the sentences with the correct words from the box.

alarming	steady	success	unemployment

1. When new jobs are created, the _____ rate is lowered.

2. DNA-testing websites claim to have a good _____ rate for decoding people's genetic ancestry.

3. The economy is continuing to grow at a slow but _____ rate.

4. Arctic sea ice is melting at a(n) _____ rate, which is bad news for global sea levels.

BEFORE YOU READ

DISCUSSION **A.** Look at the picture below and read the caption. Discuss these questions with a partner.

    1. Why do you think the Lapita decided to undertake such a risky adventure?

    2. How did the Lapita locate hundreds of distant islands scattered across the largest ocean on Earth?

SCANNING **B.** Scan the reading passage on the next four pages to see if your predictions in activity A were correct.

Scientists believe many Polynesians are descendants of an earlier group of Pacific Islanders called the Lapita who—thousands of years ago—began exploring the Pacific Ocean.

FANTASTIC
VOYAGE

A   It is mid-afternoon on the island of Bora Bora in French Polynesia. Thousands
of cheering spectators crowd the shore to see the end of the Hawaiki Nui Va'a,
a challenging 130-kilometer Polynesian canoe race that virtually stops the nation.
"This is our heritage," says Manutea Owen, a former canoe champion and a hero
on his home island of Huahine. "Our people came from over the sea by canoe.
Sometimes when I'm out there competing, I try to imagine what they must have
endured and the adventures they had crossing those huge distances."

Pioneers of the Pacific

B   Manutea Owen's ancestors colonized nearly every island in the South Pacific. This
was a remarkable feat[1] of human **navigation**—comparable with humans going to
the moon. Only recently have scientists begun to understand where these amazing
voyagers came from, and how—with simple canoes and no navigation equipment—
they reached hundreds of islands scattered across an ocean that covers nearly a third
of the globe. This expansion into the Pacific was accomplished by two extraordinary
civilizations: the Lapita and the Polynesians.

C   From about 1300 to 800 B.C., the Lapita people colonized islands that **stretch** over
millions of square kilometers, including the Solomon Islands, Vanuatu, Fiji, New
Caledonia, and Samoa. Then, for unknown reasons, they stopped. There was an

interval of around 1,000 years before the Polynesian civilization—descendants of the Lapita—launched a new period of exploration. They outdid the Lapita with unbelievable feats of navigation. They expanded the boundaries of their world until it was many times the size of that explored by their ancestors. Their colonies included the Cook Islands, French Polynesia, Hawaii, and Easter Island, eventually reaching South America around A.D. 1000.

How Did They Do It?

D There is one **stubborn** question for which archeology has yet to provide any answers. How did the Lapita and early Polynesian pioneers accomplish a feat that is **analogous** to a moon landing? Little evidence remains to help us understand their remarkable sailing skills. Unfortunately, no one has found an **intact** Lapita or early Polynesian canoe that might reveal the sailing techniques used. Nor do the oral histories[2] and traditions of later Polynesians offer any insights as to how their ancestors navigated areas of open ocean thousands of kilometers wide without becoming lost. "All we can say for certain is that the Lapita had canoes that were capable of ocean voyages, and they had the ability to sail them," says Geoff Irwin, a professor of archeology at the University of Auckland. Nonetheless, scientists have some theories about the secrets of these explorers' successes.

E Sailors have always relied upon the so-called trade winds, winds that blow steadily and in predictable directions over the ocean's surface. Irwin notes that the Lapita's expansion into the Pacific was eastward, against steady trade winds. Sailing against the wind, he argues, may have been the key to their success: "They could sail out for days into the unknown …, secure in the knowledge that if they didn't find anything,

---

1 If you refer to something as a **feat**, you admire it because it is an impressive and difficult achievement.
2 **Oral history** is the collection and study of spoken memories, stories, and songs.

ˇ **Hawaiian canoeists race in the waters of Kauai island, using a modern version of an ancient design.**

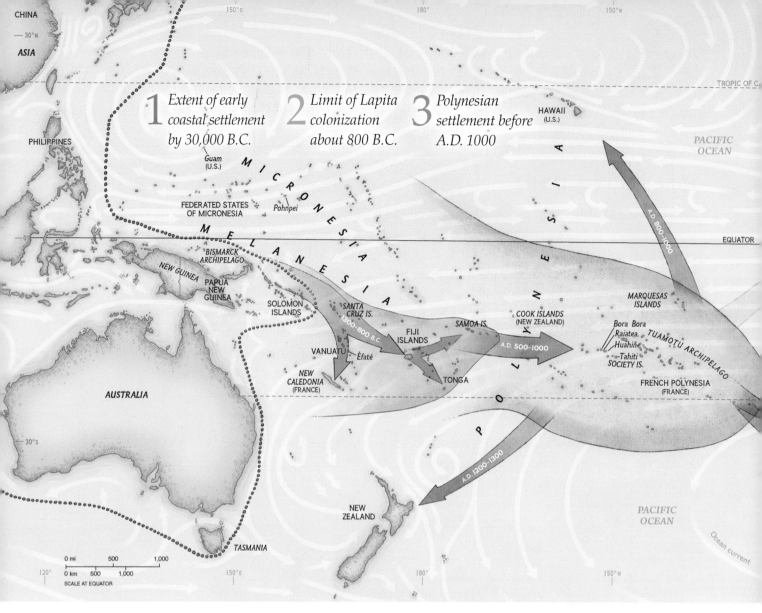

1 *Extent of early coastal settlement by 30,000 B.C.*

2 *Limit of Lapita colonization about 800 B.C.*

3 *Polynesian settlement before A.D. 1000*

The Lapita traveled east from New Guinea some 3,000 years ago, and within a few centuries reached Tonga and Samoa. A thousand years later, their Polynesian descendants pushed farther, eventually reaching the most remote islands in the Pacific.

they could turn around and catch a swift ride home on the trade winds." For returning explorers, successful or not, the geography of their own archipelagos[3] provided a safety net. It ensured that sailors wouldn't sail too far and become lost in the open ocean. Vanuatu, for example, is a chain of islands 800 kilometers long with many islands within sight of each other. Once sailors hit that string of islands, they could find their way home.

F Irwin hypothesizes that once out in the open ocean, the explorers would detect a variety of **clues** to follow to land. This included seabirds and turtles that need islands on

which to build their nests, coconuts and twigs[4] carried out to sea, and the clouds that tend to form over some islands in the afternoon. It is also possible that Lapita sailors followed the smoke from distant volcanoes to new islands.

Helped by El Niño?

G These theories rely on one unproven point— that the Lapita and early Polynesians had mastered the skill of sailing against the wind

---

3 An **archipelago** is a large group or chain of islands.

4 A **twig** is a very small, thin branch.

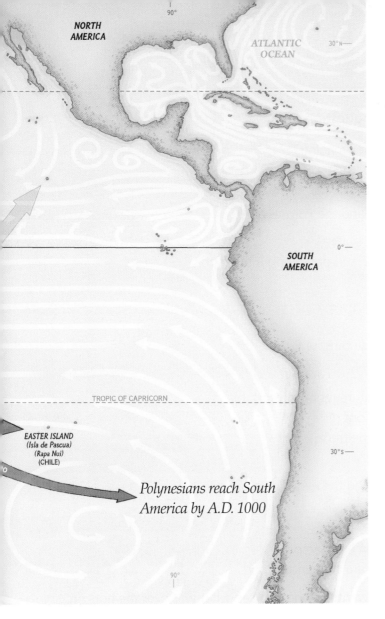

NORTH AMERICA

ATLANTIC OCEAN

SOUTH AMERICA

EASTER ISLAND
(Isla de Pascua)
(Rapa Nui)
(CHILE)

TROPIC OF CAPRICORN

Polynesians reach South America by A.D. 1000

distant voyages. Anderson believes that the Lapita may have taken advantage of trade winds blowing east instead of west, thereby voyaging far to the east without any knowledge of tacking techniques.

The success of the Lapita and their descendants may have been due to their own sailing skills, to reverse trade winds, or to a mixture of both. Or it may even have been due to facts still unknown. But it is certain that by the time Europeans came to the Pacific, nearly every piece of land—hundreds of islands in all—had already been discovered by the Lapita and the Polynesians. Exactly why these ancient peoples set out on such giant migrations remains a mystery. However, as Professor Irwin puts it, "Whatever you believe, the really fascinating part of this story isn't the methods they used, but their motives. The Lapita, for example, didn't need to pick up and go; there was nothing forcing them, no overcrowded homeland. They went because they wanted to go and see what was over the **horizon**."

using a technique called "tacking." Rather than give all the credit to their bravery and technique, Atholl Anderson of the Australian National University thinks that they might also have been lucky—helped by a weather **phenomenon** known as El Niño.

El Niño occurs in the Pacific Ocean when the surface water temperature is unusually high. It **disrupts** world weather in a variety of ways. One of its effects is to cause trade winds in the South Pacific to weaken or to reverse direction and blow to the east. Scientists believe that El Niño phenomena were unusually frequent around the time of the Lapita expansion, and again between 1,200 and 1,600 years ago, when the early Polynesians began their even more

△ **This Lapita pot was uncovered in a 3,000-year-old burial site on Efate Island, Vanuatu.**

A. Choose the best answer for each question.

GIST **1.** What could be another title for this reading?

  a. How Ancient Peoples Explored the Pacific
  b. How El Niño Helped the Lapita
  c. The Race Between the Lapita and the Polynesians
  d. An Oral History of the Lapita

REFERENCE **2.** The phrase *these amazing voyagers* in paragraph B refers to _____.

  a. men who went to the moon
  b. the Lapita and the early Polynesians
  c. today's Polynesians
  d. Manutea Owen and the people of Bora Bora

DETAIL **3.** How might El Niño have assisted early Pacific sailors?

  a. by making the water temperature more comfortable
  b. by creating calmer sea conditions
  c. by reversing the direction of the trade winds
  d. by making tacking easier

DETAIL **4.** What is true for both the Lapita and the early Polynesians?

  a. They reached South America.
  b. They may have been helped by El Niño.
  c. They colonized New Caledonia and Samoa.
  d. Their navigational techniques are well understood.

PARAPHRASE **5.** What does Irwin mean by "they wanted to go and see what was over the horizon" (paragraph I)?

  a. The Lapita were motivated by a curiosity about new places.
  b. The Lapita hoped for greater security in faraway places.
  c. The Lapita desired better living conditions on other islands.
  d. The Lapita needed to find food and fresh water overseas.

UNDERSTANDING MAPS **B.** Look back at the map on pages 90–91. Are the following statements true or false, or is the information not given? Circle **T** (true), **F** (false), or **NG** (not given).

1. Australia was already populated by 30,000 B.C.　　　　　　**T F NG**

2. The Lapita sailed as far as New Zealand.　　　　　　**T F NG**

3. The Polynesians who sailed to the Hawaiian Islands came from the Marquesas Islands.　　　　　　**T F NG**

4. Most of the islands of French Polynesia are of volcanic origin.　　　　　　**T F NG**

5. The Polynesians did not reach South America.　　　　　　**T F NG**

Distinguishing Fact from Speculation

Texts often contain a mix of facts and speculations. Facts are ideas that are known to be true, or that can be proven. A speculation is a person's guess about what they think happened; in these situations, there isn't enough information to be certain. *Speculation* and *theory* are often used as interchangeable terms. Words that usually indicate a speculation (or theory) include *believe, think, hypothesize, suggest, argue, may, might, possibly, likely,* and *perhaps*. By distinguishing fact from speculation, you will be better able to evaluate the information and ideas in a passage.

FACT OR
SPECULATION

A. Read these sentences from Reading B. For each, write **F** (fact) or **S** (speculation).

1. From about 1300 to 800 B.C., the Lapita people colonized islands that stretch over millions of square kilometers. _____

2. All we can say for certain is that the Lapita had canoes that were capable of ocean voyages, and they had the ability to sail them. _____

3. Sailing against the wind, [Irwin] argues, may have been the key to their success. _____

4. Irwin hypothesizes that once out in the open ocean, the explorers would detect a variety of clues to follow to land. _____

5. Anderson believes that the Lapita may have taken advantage of trade winds blowing east instead of west, thereby voyaging far to the east without any knowledge of tacking techniques. _____

FACT OR
SPECULATION

B. Find the information below (1–4) in Reading B. Is each presented as a fact or a speculation? Write **F** (fact) or **S** (speculation). Then circle the words in the passage that indicate the speculations.

1. Lapita sailors followed the smoke from distant volcanoes to new islands. (paragraph F) _____

2. One of El Niño's effects is to cause trade winds in the South Pacific to weaken or to reverse direction. (paragraph H) _____

3. El Niño phenomena were unusually frequent around the time of the Lapita expansion. (paragraph H) _____

4. By the time Europeans came to the Pacific, nearly every piece of land had already been discovered by the Lapita and the Polynesians. (paragraph I) _____

CRITICAL THINKING Reflecting   Discuss these questions with a partner.

▶ According to Professor Irwin, the Lapita didn't have to explore; they just wanted to "see what was over the horizon." Are there any expeditions or explorations today with similar motives? Note some ideas below.

▶ Would you like to join these kinds of expeditions? Why or why not?

COMPLETION **A.** Circle the correct words to complete the information below.

It was once widely accepted that the first people in the Americas arrived by walking across a land bridge from Siberia. They then traveled south between great sheets of ice that ¹**navigated / stretched** across North America at that time. Today, this theory is being challenged. An alternative idea suggests that instead of a single first migration, groups came at separate ²**intervals / clues**. Another theory suggests that they may have ³**disrupted / navigated** their way along the shoreline using kayaks.

The debate over this migration path is one of many disputes in the field of archeology. Evidence from the distant past is hard to find, so theories are often based on very small ⁴**clues / analogies**. As new evidence is uncovered that ⁵**navigates / disrupts** existing ideas, experts often need to adjust their theories.

⌃ **Archeologists discovered a digging stick in Chile, estimated to be 12,500 years old.**

WORDS IN CONTEXT **B.** Complete the sentences. Circle the correct words.

1. A **phenomenon** is an event that *is observable / cannot be seen*.
2. Two things are **analogous** when they are *different / similar*.
3. If an ancient pot is found **intact**, it is *broken / complete*.
4. The **horizon** is the line where the *water and shore / earth and sky* seem to meet.
5. A **stubborn** problem is *difficult / easy* to fix or deal with.

WORD PARTS **C.** The word **analogous** contains the suffix *-ous*, which means "full of" or "possessing." Add this suffix to the words in the box to complete the sentences.

continue	courage	fame

1. Bora Bora is one of the most _____ islands in French Polynesia.
2. The _____ rowing of a canoe would tire anyone out quickly.
3. Early sailors were _____ to cross such large areas of unknown ocean.

CAVE ARTISTS

Artwork on the walls of Chauvet
Cave, France, is believed to be
more than 30,000 years old.

BEFORE YOU WATCH

PREVIEWING **A.** Read the information. The words in **bold** appear in the video. Match these
words with their definitions below.

Cave paintings—or cave art—**depict** a variety of things, from animals **engraved** in the
rock to hand stencils made by placing a hand on the wall and blowing **pigment** at it.
At around 40,000 B.C., cave artists **predominantly** drew and painted large predator
species, but by around 25,000 B.C., hunted animals became the favorite theme. Some
of the animals depicted in cave art are now extinct.

1. depict   •   • a. a colored powder used to make paint

2. engrave   •   • b. mainly; for the most part

3. pigment   •   • c. to represent in a drawing or painting

4. predominantly •   • d. to cut or carve words or pictures into the surface
of a hard object

DISCUSSION **B.** Why do you think our ancient ancestors made these kinds of images on cave
walls? Discuss with a partner and note some ideas.

_____

_____

GIST **A. Watch the video. Check (✓) the questions that are answered in the video.**

☐ a. Where are art-filled caves predominantly located?

☐ b. How old is cave art?

☐ c. Who discovered the first cave painting?

☐ d. How was cave art created?

☐ e. What steps are researchers taking to preserve cave paintings?

☐ f. What can we learn from cave art?

COMPLETION **B. Watch the video again and complete the notes below.**

Ancient cave art

- predominantly found in France and 1_____

- scientific testing has revealed most art to be less than 2_____ years old

- mostly depicts animals that humans would have encountered during the 3_____ Age

- mostly created using red or 4_____ pigments made from rocks

- repeated symbols may represent the earliest form of graphic 5_____

CRITICAL THINKING Reflecting   Consider what you have learned in this unit. Do you think that studying early human migration patterns and ancient cave art is worth the time and effort? Why or why not? Note your ideas below and share with a partner.

_____

_____

VOCABULARY REVIEW

Do you remember the meanings of these words? Check (✓) the ones you know. Look back at the unit and review any words you're not sure of.

Reading A

☐ bulk*   ☐ calculate   ☐ descendant   ☐ identical*   ☐ immense

☐ rate   ☐ roughly   ☐ scattered   ☐ trace*   ☐ vanish

Reading B

☐ analogous*   ☐ clue   ☐ disrupt   ☐ horizon   ☐ intact

☐ interval*   ☐ navigation   ☐ phenomenon*   ☐ stretch   ☐ stubborn

* Academic Word List

MONEY AND TRADE

6

^ Ancient coins are among the
treasures recovered from a
300-year-old shipwreck.

97

6A

BEFORE YOU READ

DEFINITIONS   **A.** The following money-related words appear in the reading passage. Use the words to complete the definitions (1–4).

bill   credit card   foreign exchange   inflation

1. _____ is an increase in the prices of goods and services.
2. _____ is the conversion of one country's currency into another.
3. A(n) _____ is a small piece of material, usually plastic, that can be used to pay for something.
4. A(n) _____ is a piece of paper money.

PREDICTING   **B.** What methods of payment do you think people used in ancient times? Discuss with a partner. Check your ideas as you read the passage.

❯ **Workers inspect an enlarged U.S. $100 bill against counterfeit sections.**

HOW MONEY MADE US MODERN

A   About 9,500 years ago, ancient accountants in Sumer[1] invented a way to keep track of farmers' crops and livestock. They began using small pieces of baked clay, almost like the tokens used in board games today. One piece might **signify** a measure of grain, while another with a different shape might represent a farm animal or a jar of olive oil.

B   Those little ceramic shapes might not seem to have much in common with today's $100 bill—or with the credit cards and online **transactions** that are rapidly taking the place of cash—but the roots of our modern methods of **payment** lie in those Sumerian tokens. Such early accounting tools evolved into a system of finance and into money itself: a symbolic representation of value that can be transferred from one person to another as payment for goods or services.

The Rise of Gold

C   Since ancient times, humans have used items to represent value—from stones to animal skins, to whale teeth. In the ancient world, people often relied upon symbols that had tangible[2] value in their own right. The ancient Chinese made payments with cowrie shells,[3] which were prized for their beauty as materials for jewelry. As Glyn Davies notes in his book *A History of Money from Ancient Times to the Present Day*, cowrie shells are durable, easily cleaned and counted, and defy imitation or counterfeiting.[4]

D   But eventually there arose a new, universal currency: gold. The gleaming metal could be combined with other metals at high temperatures to create alloys,[5] and was easy to melt and hammer into shapes. It became the raw material for the first coins, created in Lydia (present-day Turkey) around 2,700 years ago. Lydian coins didn't look much like today's coinage. They were irregular in shape and size and didn't have values inscribed on them; instead, they used a stamped image to indicate their weight and value.

E   The result, explains financial author Kabir Sehgal, was an economic system in which "you knew the value of what you had, and what you could buy with it." Unlike modern money, ancient coins were what economists call full-bodied or **commodity** money: Their value was fixed by the metal in them.

---

1   **Sumer** was a region of ancient Mesopotamia in what is now Iraq and Kuwait.
2   If something is **tangible**, it is real or can be touched.
3   **Cowrie shells** are smooth, shiny, egg-shaped seashells.
4   **Counterfeiting** refers to creating fake money or documents.
5   An **alloy** is a metal made by mixing two metals together.

A shopper pays with cash at Sri Lanka's Pettah Market.

The Birth of Trade

F Money's **convenience** made it easier for ancient merchants to develop large-scale trade networks, in which spices and grain could be bought and sold across distances of thousands of kilometers. This led to the first foreign exchanges: In the ancient Greek city-state of Corinth, banks were set up where foreign traders could exchange their own coins for Corinthian ones.

G In the centuries that followed, trade routes forged more cultural connections between nations and regions. Besides exchanging money and goods, traders also spread religious beliefs, knowledge, and new inventions, creating connections among far-flung cultures.

H The dangers of moving money and goods over distances—whether from storms at sea or bandits and pirates—led humans to develop increasingly complex economic organizations. In the 1600s, investors gathering in London coffeehouses began to underwrite[6] traders and colonists heading to the New World, financing their voyages in exchange for a share of the crops or goods they brought back. Investors tried to reduce their risk by buying shares of multiple ventures. It was the start of a global economy in which vast quantities of products and money began to flow across borders in search of profit.

Notes and Bills

I By the 1700s, the global economy had grown so much that it was inconvenient to transport and store large quantities of coins. Several societies therefore shifted toward paper currency. The earliest paper bills were literally receipts that gave the bearer[7] ownership of gold or silver coins that could be collected upon demand.

J But as Lloyd Thomas explains in his book *Money, Banking and Financial Markets*, bankers eventually realized that many people simply used their notes rather than redeeming them for gold. It meant that the bankers didn't actually need to have enough gold on hand to

---

6 If a company **underwrites** an activity, it agrees to provide money to cover any losses.

7 The **bearer** of a document is the person who owns it.

cover all the notes they issued. That revelation, Thomas says, eventually led to the concept of fiat money, which governments issue today. In contrast to commodity money, today's money has value **essentially** because a government says that it does. Its purchasing power remains relatively **stable** because the government controls the supply. That's why a U.S. $100 bill is worth $100, even though it only contains a few cents worth of raw materials.

K It's a system with an important advantage, in that human **judgment**—rather than how much gold has been dug out of the ground—determines the amount of money in circulation. On the other hand, this can become a disadvantage. If a government decides to issue too much money, it can **trigger** an inflationary spiral that raises the price of goods and services.

Toward Virtual Money

L By the 20th century, new methods of payment had begun to emerge as alternatives to cash. In the 1920s, oil companies and hotel chains began to issue credit cards: These enabled customers to make purchases and pay

what they owed later. In 1950, Diners Club International issued the first universal credit card, which could be used to purchase things at a variety of places. Using plastic to make purchases eventually proved more convenient than bills, coins, or even checks.

M In 2009, yet another high-tech successor to money emerged: Bitcoin. Bitcoins are a sort of unofficial virtual Internet currency. They aren't issued or even controlled by governments, and they exist only in the cloud or on a person's computer. Parag Khanna, a financial **policy** expert, explains: "The real future is technology as money. That's what Bitcoin is about."

N From the clay tokens of Sumer to today's virtual currencies, the evolution of money has helped drive the development of civilization. Money makes it easier not only to buy and sell goods, but also to connect with the world, enabling traders to roam across continents, and investors to amass wealth. It is a type of language that we all speak. From the humblest shop clerk to the wealthiest Wall Street financier, money exerts a powerful influence upon us all.

The gold vault at the New York Federal Reserve contains 5 percent of the world's gold.

A. Choose the best answer for each question.

GIST **1.** What is the best alternative title for the passage?

a. How Paper Money Changed the World
b. From Ceramic Tokens to Bitcoin: The Evolution of Money
c. Ancient Sumer and the Origins of Trading
d. A Return to Commodity Money

DETAIL **2.** The writer says that ancient Sumerian tokens ____ .

a. were all the same shape
b. were made of different materials
c. had to be heated in order to harden them
d. resembled modern board game pieces

An ancient coin of the Seleucid Empire

MAIN IDEA **3.** According to the writer, gatherings in London coffeehouses in the 1600s ____ .

a. represented the first form of banking
b. led to the first foreign currency exchanges
c. helped bring about the global economy
d. resulted in a general move toward commodity money

DETAIL **4.** A $100 bill is an example of ____ money.

a. commodity   c. fiat
b. virtual   d. universal

INFERENCE **5.** Who is most likely to agree that physical money will be replaced in the near future?

a. Parag Khanna   c. Kabir Sehgal
b. Glyn Davies   d. Lloyd Thomas

CLASSIFYING **B. Do the following characteristics describe commodity money or fiat money? Complete the chart with the correct information (a–g).**

a. may involve objects that are regarded as beautiful
b. is the currency system now in use in most economies
c. was the currency system used in ancient Lydia
d. is valuable only because the government says it is valuable
e. is also known as "full-bodied" money
f. may contain precious metals such as gold
g. is made of materials that have little actual value

Commodity Money	Fiat Money

Understanding the Function of Sentences

As you read, try to identify the purpose, or function, of individual sentences. This can help you understand the overall organization of a text. Here are some common functions of sentences.

Defining: Sumerian tokens were an early form of money.
Classifying: There are two types of money: commodity and fiat.
Quoting: As economist Maynard Keynes said, "Ideas shape the course of history."
Reporting: According to archeologists, the first money was Sumerian tokens.
Cause-Effect: Today's money has value because a government says that it does.
Condition: If you heat gold, it melts easily, making it ideal for creating coins.
Naming: The first universal credit card was the Diners Club card.

UNDERSTANDING FUNCTION

A. Write the function of each sentence. Use the functions in the box above.

1. But eventually there arose a new, universal currency: gold. _____
2. The result, explains financial author Kabir Sehgal, was an economic system in which "you knew the value of what you had, and what you could buy with it." _____
3. Cowrie shells are smooth, shiny, egg-shaped seashells. _____
4. But as Lloyd Thomas explains in his book *Money, Banking and Financial Markets*, bankers eventually realized that many people simply used their notes rather than redeeming them for gold. _____
5. Its purchasing power remains relatively stable because the government controls the supply. _____
6. If a government decides to issue too much money, it can trigger an inflationary spiral that raises the price of goods and services. _____

UNDERSTANDING FUNCTION

B. Look back at paragraph M in Reading A. Underline sentences that match three of the functions in the box above. What is the function of each underlined sentence?

CRITICAL THINKING Evaluating Pros and Cons   Discuss these questions with a partner.

▶ What do you think are the pros and cons for a country to "go cashless"? Note some ideas.

Pros: _____
_____

Cons: _____
_____

▶ Which types of transactions or activities do you think are most likely to go cashless first? Give reasons for your answers.

COMPLETION **A.** Complete the paragraph with words from the box.

convenience	judged	payment
policy	transactions	trigger

Sweden will soon become a cashless society. This means that cash will no longer be accepted as ¹_____ for goods and services. Many Swedes already appreciate the ²_____ of not having to carry cash. Currently, 80 percent of all ³_____ are electronic, with most consumers using a credit card or cell phone app. The government thinks the new ⁴_____ will also cut down on tax cheats, and reduce crime. If Sweden's move is ⁵_____ a success, it could ⁶_____ a wave of other countries abandoning cash entirely.

A customer in Sweden pays for food using a phone app.

WORDS IN CONTEXT **B.** Complete the sentences. Circle the correct words.

1. An economy with low inflation and *fairly constant / unsteady* growth is considered to be relatively **stable**.

2. Examples of **commodities** include *love and friendship / oil and natural gas*.

3. You might **signify** your agreement by *nodding your head / thinking to yourself*.

4. If something is **essentially** true, it is *basically / entirely* true.

COLLOCATIONS **C.** The words in the box are often used with the noun **policy**. Complete the sentences with the correct words from the box.

company	insurance	public	strict

1. Nearly all airlines have a very _____ no-smoking policy on flights.

2. If you purchase a car, you usually need to take out a(n) _____ policy.

3. Most businesses have their own _____ policy regarding working hours.

4. Health care and education are usually areas of _____ policy.

BEFORE YOU READ

QUIZ **A.** Complete these sentences. Then check your answers on page 114.

1. The average lifespan of a U.S. $1 bill is six *months / years / decades*.

2. There is a total of about $1.5 *million / billion / trillion* in U.S. physical currency in circulation.

3. Physical currency makes up *11 / 33 / 80* percent of the total money supply in the U.S.

PREDICTING **B.** Read the introduction to the passage on page 107. What do you know about virtual currency? What might be some pros and cons of using it? Discuss with a partner, and check your ideas as you read the passage.

∨ A collection of coins representing Bitcoin, a type of virtual currency

> Technicians inspect a
Bitcoin mining facility in
Saint-Hyacinthe, Canada.

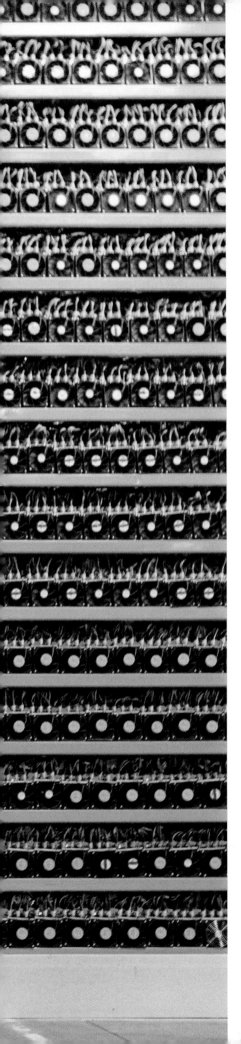

THE RISE OF VIRTUAL MONEY

It doesn't exist in any physical form, yet is increasingly used by people worldwide. Is virtual currency the money of the future?

What Is a Virtual Currency?

A   According to the European Banking Authority, a virtual currency is "a digital representation of value that is neither issued by a central bank or a public authority, nor necessarily attached to a fiat currency, but is accepted [as] a means of payment and can be transferred, stored, or traded electronically." There are many types of virtual currency, but the best known is probably Bitcoin.

B   In online articles, or in newspapers or magazines, you may have seen pictures of gold or silver coins marked with the Bitcoin symbol (₿). However—since Bitcoins exist only as digital constructs—these are merely representations. Bitcoin is a type of digital money known as a "cryptocurrency"; that is, it uses cryptography—secure coding—to **verify** ownership of the money. The money can be sent electronically from one user to another anywhere in the world.

C   Unlike traditional currencies, Bitcoin is not controlled by a central bank or by a government agency. And unlike credit cards, the Bitcoin network is not run by a company. There is no middleman between the parties that are transferring money. It is operated by a global network of computers called a blockchain network, which records every Bitcoin transaction in the world.

How Did Bitcoin Begin?

D   The first reference to Bitcoin appeared in 2008, in a paper by a writer **supposedly** named Satoshi Nakamoto. However, the name turned out to be a pseudonym[1] for a person or group who preferred to remain anonymous. A year later, Bitcoin was released as open-source software.

---

1 A **pseudonym** is a name that someone uses in place of their real name.

E Bitcoin was not the first attempt at a cryptocurrency; others had existed in one form or another for nearly 50 years, but without much success. In a short space of time, though, Bitcoin became the first cryptocurrency to be widely traded internationally. The first Bitcoins were mined in January 2009; within 200 days, one million coins had been mined. By 2019, this had risen to over 17 million Bitcoins—worth a total of U.S. $65 billion—and more than 300,000 new transactions were taking place every day.

F In its early days, Bitcoin was known for its link with illegal **drugs**, such as those bought and sold on Silk Road, an online black market set up in 2011. Silk Road connected customers and sellers on the Internet using a network that concealed a user's location and identity—and it used Bitcoin for payments. Silk Road was shut down by the FBI[2] in 2013. According to some experts, the shutdown gave Bitcoin a chance to gain some much-needed legitimacy. BitPay CEO Stephen Pair insisted that Silk Road's association would not prove fatal to Bitcoin. He said that the shutdown "shows that just because you use Bitcoin doesn't mean you can evade law enforcement."

How Does Bitcoin Work?

G Each Bitcoin can be divided out to eight decimal places. That means you can send someone a minimum of 0.00000001 Bitcoins. This smallest fraction of a Bitcoin—the penny of the Bitcoin world—is called a "Satoshi."

H Like gold or other precious metals used as money, Bitcoins are **scarce**. But their scarcity is not natural or accidental. New Bitcoins are added only by being "mined." Computer users on the blockchain network race to solve increasingly complicated mathematical problems. The first to have a verified solution receives a payment. It's like the high-tech equivalent of a gold rush.[3] The mined Bitcoin can then be traded using special computer software.

I A useful analogy: Think of the blockchain network as an engine. Engines can be used to power all types of vehicles: cars, boats, aircraft. Bitcoin is a vehicle that uses that engine. Because it was the first major virtual currency to use blockchain, you could think of Bitcoin as an early model vehicle, like a Model T Ford.[4] More **sophisticated** uses of this engine may occur in the future.

What Are the Benefits of Using a Virtual Currency Like Bitcoin?

J In most cases, financial transactions involve exchange fees, taxes, and payment delays to guard against **fraud**. Virtual transactions, however, are speedy and cheap—and are settled immediately. And unlike a credit card exchange, where credit card numbers and security information are handed over completely for any transaction, a Bitcoin transfer is authorized only to pay a specific amount.

K Virtual currencies also make it possible to make a digital payment without needing PayPal or a credit card. This is particularly useful in many parts of Africa, Latin America, and South Asia. Immigrants to developed countries may find it a convenient way to send funds back home to their families.

L Bitcoin supporter Jonathan Mohan says, "The vast majority of [people on] the planet don't even own a bank account … Just as in Africa, [people] went directly to cell phones. In these developing nations, you're not going to see them start getting bank accounts. You're going to see them just going straight to Bitcoins."

---

2 The **FBI** (Federal Bureau of Investigation) is a government agency in the United States that investigates crimes.

3 A **gold rush** is a situation in which a lot of people move to a place where gold has been discovered to try to find gold there (e.g., the California Gold Rush of 1849).

4 A **Model T Ford** was an early model automobile, first sold in 1908.

Bitcoin in Perspective

The global market share for cryptocurrencies can grow a lot more

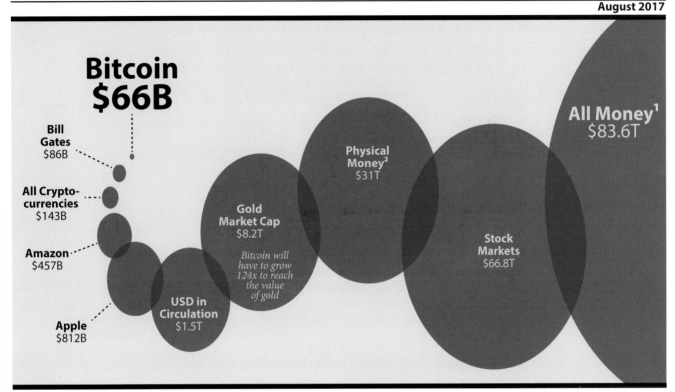

Bitcoin $66B

Bill Gates $86B

All Crypto-currencies $143B

Amazon $457B

Apple $812B

USD in Circulation $1.5T

Gold Market Cap $8.2T

Bitcoin will have to grow 124x to reach the value of gold

Physical Money[2] $31T

Stock Markets $66.8T

All Money[1] $83.6T

Sources:
https://howmuch.net/articles/worlds-money-in-perspective
https://coinmarketcap.com
https://www.forbes.com
https://www.federalreserve.gov
https://www.cia.gov

Adapted from Bitcoin IRA.

Diagram not to scale.

[1]**All Money** = money in any form including bank or other deposits, as well as notes and coins.
[2]**Physical Money** = money in forms that can be used as a medium of exchange; generally notes, coins, and certain balances held by banks.

What Are the Drawbacks of Bitcoin?

M The most obvious **drawback** is a lack of stability in the value of the currency. Bitcoin's independence makes it more stable in **principle** than traditional currencies. In reality, though, its value has fluctuated wildly over the time it has been in existence. In 2012, the price of a Bitcoin was about U.S. $12; by December 2015, it had reached U.S. $400.

Two years later, it reached a peak of almost U.S. $20,000, but then lost almost 80 percent of that value within a year. Those are some wild swings.

N So it is worth thinking twice before putting all or a substantial amount of your **assets** into a virtual currency like Bitcoin. The rule of investing in virtual currency is the same as investing in **stocks**: Never invest more than you can afford to lose.

A. Choose the best answer for each question.

MAIN IDEA

1. Which of the following statements is NOT true?

a. Bitcoin transactions are made without middlemen.

b. New Bitcoins are made by users in a computer network.

c. The value of Bitcoins is controlled by a central bank.

d. Bitcoins are created through a process known as mining.

DETAIL

2. The pictures mentioned in the first sentence of paragraph B _____.

a. are images of old Bitcoins

b. do not represent real objects

c. show future versions of Bitcoins

d. are photos of ancient gold coins

PURPOSE

3. What is the main purpose of paragraph C?

a. to discuss different types of cryptocurrencies

b. to trace the early history of Bitcoin

c. to contrast Bitcoin with other methods of payment

d. to compare traditional currencies and credit cards

DETAIL

4. According to the passage, which of the following is NOT true about Silk Road?

a. It was in operation for about two years.

b. Its shutdown may actually have helped Bitcoin.

c. It continues to operate today under another name.

d. It made use of the Internet and Bitcoin.

INFERENCE

5. According to the analogy in paragraph I, a supersonic jet plane would represent _____.

a. an advanced form of virtual currency

b. a new type of blockchain network

c. one of today's cryptocurrencies

d. a different way to mine Bitcoins

EVALUATING STATEMENTS

B. Are the following statements true or false according to the reading passage, or is the information not given? Circle **T** (true), **F** (false), or **NG** (not given).

1. Satoshi Nakamoto may have been more than one person.   **T F NG**

2. Before Bitcoin, earlier attempts at creating cryptocurrencies had failed due to lack of public trust.   **T F NG**

3. The value of a Satoshi is more than the value of a Bitcoin.   **T F NG**

4. Jonathan Mohan predicts that Bitcoin will be popular in Africa.   **T F NG**

5. From 2015 to 2017, the value of Bitcoin increased significantly.   **T F NG**

6. Switzerland is one of the most Bitcoin-friendly countries in the world.   **T F NG**

Summarizing (2)—Creating an Outline

As you learned in Unit 2A, a concept map is a common method of summarizing a passage; another method is to create an outline. A traditional outline uses roman numerals (I, II, III) for main ideas, capital letters (A, B, C) for subtopics, numbers (1, 2, 3) for supporting facts, and lower-case letters (a, b, c) for additional details. Alternatively, bullets can be used for the supporting facts and details. Indenting the information can also help to show the relative importance of ideas.

OUTLINING **A.** Look back at paragraphs A–F in Reading B. Then complete the outline below with words, phrases, or numbers from the reading passage.

OUTLINE: The Rise of Virtual Money

I. What is virtual money?
    A. Definition
        1. A digital representation of value
        2. Not issued by a central ^{1}_____ or public authority
        3. Can be transferred, stored, or traded ^{2}_____
    B. Bitcoin
        1. A type of virtual money that uses secure ^{3}_____ to verify ownership
        2. Operated by a ^{4}_____ network (global computer network)

II. How did Bitcoin begin?
    A. Early days
        1. First mined in January ^{5}_____; fast growth
        2. First cryptocurrency to be widely traded internationally
    B. Early uses
        1. Known for its link with illegal ^{6}_____
        2. Associated with an online black market called ^{7}_____

OUTLINING **B.** Now look back at paragraphs G–N in Reading B. Highlight the most important information. Then create an outline.

CRITICAL THINKING Reflecting   Some companies have started paying their employees in Bitcoin. Would you like to be paid in Bitcoin? Why or why not? Note your answer and reasons below. Then discuss with a partner.

_____

_____

COMPLETION **A. Complete the information with words from the box.**

> **drawback   principles   scarce   sophisticated   verify**

Cryptocurrencies like Bitcoin seem very ¹_____, but they have some simple and ancient origins, says archeologist Scott Fitzpatrick. In fact, Bitcoin shares similarities with the famous limestone coins found on the Micronesian island of Yap.

Several hundred years ago, the Yapese used some of the same ²_____ as Bitcoin in order to conduct business. Limestone was ³_____ on Yap, so the islanders traveled to nearby islands to mine it—similar to how new Bitcoins are "mined" through mathematical processes. Bitcoin transactions are recorded on the public blockchain; similarly, the Yapese stored their stone money in public places where villagers could inspect and ⁴_____ its quality.

⌃ **A Yapese boy stands next to stone money.**

One ⁵_____ of Yap's money was its large size, so the islanders pioneered a public system for "exchanging" it. The stones changed ownership without being physically moved. Bitcoin, too, changes ownership without an actual exchange of physical currency.

WORDS IN CONTEXT **B. Complete the sentences. Circle the correct words.**

1. A **drug** is something someone might put *on their head / in their body*.
2. If something **supposedly** happened, it *definitely / may have* happened.
3. If someone commits **fraud**, they may *go to jail / get an award*.
4. Your **assets** are things that you *own / feel*.
5. When you buy **stocks**, you purchase *property / part of a company*.

WORD USAGE **C. The word principle is often confused with *principal*. A principle is a rule or law. As an adjective, principal means "the most important," and as a noun, a principal is the person in charge of a school. Circle the correct word to complete each sentence.**

1. The school *principle / principal* gave a short speech on the first day of class.
2. He is a man of great *principle / principal*.
3. The *principle / principal* export of Saudi Arabia is oil.

As an experiment, a box of money is left unattended in a public place. How would most people react?

VIDEO

TAKE THE MONEY... AND RUN?

$ FREE MONEY!

BEFORE YOU WATCH

PREVIEWING **A.** Look at the photo and caption above. Then read the extracts from the video below. Match the words and phrases in **bold** with their definitions (1–4).

"Would people's distrust keep them from taking advantage of a **no-strings-attached**, guaranteed-win situation?"

"… the money was gone **in a flash**."

"People just aren't trusting. They just assume that there's a **catch**."

"… it reflects something deep and **innate** inside of them."

1. _____ : a hidden problem or difficulty

2. _____ : very quickly

3. _____ : existing from birth; natural

4. _____ : having no special conditions or limits on an agreement or situation

MAIN IDEA **A.** Watch the video. What was the main result of the experiment? Choose the best option.

    a. Most people only took small amounts of free money.

    b. People took free money when they saw others doing so.

    c. People didn't take free money if they felt they were being watched.

COMPLETION **B.** Watch the video again and complete the chart below.

What the host did	How people reacted
• He stood in the booth and ^{1}_____	Some people ^{2}_____, but most people did not.
• He then went away and left the ^{3}_____ unattended.	Most people ^{4}_____ _____
• Finally, he placed a poster of ^{5}_____ in the booth.	^{6}_____ _____

CRITICAL THINKING Reflecting   Discuss these questions with a partner.

▸ How do you think you would have reacted to each stage of the experiment in the video?

▸ Would the results of the experiment change in different cultures? If so, how?

VOCABULARY REVIEW

Do you remember the meanings of these words? Check (✓) the ones you know. Look back at the unit and review any words you're not sure of.

Reading A

☐ commodity*   ☐ convenience   ☐ essentially   ☐ judgment   ☐ payment

☐ policy*   ☐ signify*   ☐ stable*   ☐ transaction   ☐ trigger*

Reading B

☐ asset   ☐ drawback   ☐ drug   ☐ fraud   ☐ principle*

☐ scarce   ☐ sophisticated   ☐ stocks   ☐ supposedly   ☐ verify

* Academic Word List

Answers to the Quiz on page 105: 1. years; **2.** trillion; **3.** 11

Photo and Illustration Credits

Text Credits

Acknowledgments

The Authors and Publisher would like to thank the following teaching professionals for their valuable feedback during the development of the series.

Akiko Hagiwara, Tokyo University of Pharmacy and Life Sciences; **Albert Lehner**, University of Fukui; **Alexander Cameron**, Kyushu Sangyo University; **Amira Traish**, University of Sharjah; **Andrés López**, Colégio José Max León; **Andrew Gallacher**, Kyushu Sangyo University; **Angelica Hernandez**, Liceo San Agustin; **Angus Painter**, Fukuoka University; **Anouchka Rachelson**, Miami Dade College; **Ari Hayakawa**, Aoyama Gakuin University; **Atsuko Otsuki**, Senshu University; **Ayako Hisatsune**, Kanazawa Institute of Technology; **Bogdan Pavliy**, Toyama University of International Studies; **Braden Chase**, The Braden Chase Company; **Brian J. Damm**, Kanda Institute of Foreign Languages; **Carol Friend**, Mercer County Community College; **Catherine Yu**, CNC Language School; **Chad Godfrey**, Saitama Medical University; **Chen, I-Ching**, Wenzao Ursuline University of Languages; **Cheng-hao Weng**, SMIC Private School; **Chisako Nakamura**, Ryukoku University; **Chiyo Myojin**, Kochi University of Technology; **Chris Valvona**, Okinawa Christian College; **Claire DeFord**, Olympic College; **Davi Sukses**, Sutomo 1; **David Farnell**, Fukuoka University; **David Johnson**, Kyushu Sangyo University; **Debbie Sou**, Kwong Tai Middle School; **Devin Ferreira**, University of Central Florida; **Eden Kaiser**, Framingham State University; **Ellie Park**, CNC Language School; **Elvis Bartra García**, Corporación Educativa Continental; **Emiko Yamada**, Westgate Corporation; **Eri Tamura**, Ishikawa Prefectural University; **Fadwa Sleiman**, University of Sharjah; **Frank Gutsche**, Tohoku University; **Frank Lin**, Guangzhou Tufu Culture; **Gavin Young**, Iwate University; **Gerry Landers**, GA Tech Language Institute; **Ghada Ahmed**, University of Bahrain; **Grace Choi**, Grace English School; **Greg Bevan**, Fukuoka University; **Gregg McNabb**, Shizuoka Institute of Science and Technology; **Helen Roland**, Miami Dade College; **Hersong Tang**, Shih Chien University; **Hiroshi Ohashi**, Kyushu University; **Hiroyo Yoshida**, Toyo University; **Hojin Song**, GloLink Education; **HuangFu Yen-Fang**, Tainan University of Technology; **Huey-Jye You**, NTUST; **Jackie Bae**, Plato Language School; **Jade Wong**, Belilios Public School; **James McCarron**, Chiba University; **Jane Kirsch**, INTO George Mason University; **Jenay Seymore**, Hong Ik University; **Joanne Reid**, Shin Min Senior High School; **John Appleby**, Kanda Institute of Foreign Languages; **John Nevara**, Kagoshima University; **Jonathan Bronson**, Approach International Student Center; **Joseph Zhou**, UUabc; **Josh Brunotte**, Aichi Prefectural University; **Junjun Zhou**, Menaul School; **Kaori Yamamoto**; **Katarina Zorkic**, Rosemead College; **Keiko Miyagawa**, Meiji University; **Kevin Tang**, Ritsumeikan Asia Pacific University; **Kieran Julian**, Kanda Institute of Foreign Languages; **Kim Kawashima**, Olympic College; **Kyle Kumataka**, Ritsumeikan Asia Pacific University; **Kyosuke Shimamura**, Kurume University; **Lance Stilp**, Ritsumeikan Asia Pacific University; **Li Zhaoli**, Weifang No.7 Middle School; **Lichu Lin**, NCCU; **Liza Armstrong**, University of Missouri; **Lucas Pignolet**, Ritsumeikan Asia Pacific University; **Luke Harrington**, Chiba University; **M. Lee**, KCC; **Maiko Berger**, Ritsumeikan Asia Pacific University; **Mandy Kan**, CNEC Christian College; **Mari Nakamura**, English Square; **Masako Kikukawa**, Doshisha University; **Matthew Fraser**, Westgate Corporation; **Mayuko Matsunuma**, Seijo University; **Mei-ho Chiu**, Soochow University; **Melissa Potts**, ELS Berkeley; **Michiko Imai**, Aichi University; **Monica Espinoza**, Torrance Adult School; **Ms. Manassara Riensumettharadol**, Kasetsart University; **My Uyen Tran**, Ho Chi Minh City University of Foreign Languages and Information Technology; **Nae-Dong Yang**, NTU; **Narahiko Inoue**, Kyushu University; **Neil Witkin**, Kyushu Sangyo University; **Noriko Tomioka**, Kwansei University; **Olesya Shatunova**, Kanagawa University; **Patricia Fiene**, Midwestern Career College; **Patricia Nation**, Miami Dade College; **Patrick John Johnston**, Ritsumeikan Asia Pacific University; **Paul Hansen**, Hokkaido University; **Paula Snyder**, University of Missouri-Columbia; **Ping Zhang**, Beijing Royal School; **Reiko Kachi**, Aichi University / Chukyo University; **Robert Dykes**, Jin-ai University; **Rosanna Bird**, Approach International Student Center; **Ryo Takahira**, Kurume Fusetsu High School; **Sadie Wang**, Feng Chia University; **Samuel Taylor**, Kyushu Sangyo University; **Sandra Stein**, American University of Kuwait; **Sanooch Nathalang**, Thammasat University; **Sara Sulko**, University of Missouri; **Serena Lo**, Wong Shiu Chi Secondary School; **Shih-Sheng Kuo**, NPUST; **Shin Okada**, Osaka University; **Silvana Carlini**, Colégio Agostiniano Mendel; **Silvia Yafai**, ADVETI: Applied Tech High School; **Stella Millikan**, Fukuoka Women's University; **Summer Webb**, University of Colorado Boulder; **Susumu Hiramatsu**, Okayama University; **Suzanne Littlewood**, Zayed University; **Takako Kuwayama**, Kansai University; **Takashi Urabe**, Aoyama-Gakuin University; **Teo Kim**, OROMedu; **Tim Chambers**; **Toshiya Tanaka**, Kyushu University; **Trevor Holster**, Fukuoka University; **Wakako Takinami**, Tottori University; **Wayne Malcolm**, Fukui University of Technology; **Wendy Wish**, Valencia College; **Xiaoying Zhan**, Beijing Royal Foreign Language School; **Xingwu Chen**, Xueersi-TAL; **Yin Wang**, TAL Education Group; **Yohei Murayama**, Kagoshima University; **Yoko Sakurai**, Aichi University; **Yoko Sato**, Tokyo University of Agriculture and Technology; **Yoon-Ji Ahn**, Daks Education; **Yu-Lim Im**, Daks Education; **Yuriko Ueda**, Ryukoku University; **Yvonne Hodnett**, Australian College of Kuwait; **Yvonne Johnson**, UWCSEA Dover; **Zhang Lianzhong**, Beijing Foreign Studies University

These words are used in *Reading Explorer* to describe various reading and critical thinking skills.

Analyze	to study a text in detail, e.g., to identify key points, similarities, and differences
Apply	to think about how an idea might be useful in other ways, e.g., solutions to a problem
Classify	to arrange things in groups or categories, based on their characteristics
Evaluate	to examine different sides of an issue, e.g., reasons for and against something
Infer	to "read between the lines"—information the writer expresses indirectly
Interpret	to think about what a writer means by a certain phrase or expression
Justify	to give reasons for a personal opinion, belief, or decision
Rank	to put things in order based on criteria, e.g., size or importance
Reflect	to think deeply about what a writer is saying and how it compares with your own views
Relate	to consider how ideas in a text connect with your own personal experience
Scan	to look through a text to find particular words or information
Skim	to look at a text quickly to get an overall understanding of its main idea
Summarize	to give a brief statement of the main points of a text
Synthesize	to use information from more than one source to make a judgment or comparison

INDEX OF EXAM QUESTION TYPES

The activities in *Reading Explorer, Third Edition* provide comprehensive practice of several question types that feature in standardized tests such as TOEFL® and IELTS.

Common Question Types	IELTS	TOEFL®	Page(s)
Multiple choice (gist, main idea, detail, reference, inference, vocabulary, paraphrasing)	✓	✓	12, 20, 31, 38, 48, 56, 67, 74, 84, 92, 102, 110
Completion (notes, diagram, chart)	✓		32, 42, 57, 60, 96, 111, 114
Short answer	✓		21
Matching headings / information	✓		12, 68, 74
Categorizing (matching features)	✓	✓	56, 67, 102
True / False / Not Given	✓		31, 48, 78, 92, 110
Rhetorical purpose		✓	20, 56, 74, 110

The following tips will help you become a more successful reader.

1 Preview the text

Before you start reading a text, it's important to have some idea of the overall topic. Look at the title, photos, captions, and any maps or infographics. Skim the text quickly, and scan for any key words before reading in detail.

2 Use vocabulary strategies

Here are some strategies to use if you find a word or phrase you're not sure of:

- **Look for definitions** of new words within the reading passage itself.
- **Identify the part of speech and use context** to guess the meaning of homonyms and new words or idioms (see page 13).
- **Identify the word roots and affixes** (if any) of new words.
- **Use a dictionary** if you need, but be careful to identify the correct definition.

3 Take notes

Note-taking helps you identify the main ideas and details within a text. It also helps you stay focused while reading. Try different ways of organizing your notes, and decide on a method that best suits you.

4 Infer information

Not everything is stated directly within a text. Use your own knowledge, and clues in the text, to make your own inferences and "read between the lines."

5 Make connections

As you read, look for words that help you understand how different ideas connect. For example:

- words that signal **cause and effect** (see page 49)
- words that indicate **sequence**
- words that indicate a **speculation or theory** (see page 93)

6 Read critically

Ask yourself questions as you read a text. For example, if the author presents a point of view, are enough supporting reasons or examples provided? Is the evidence reliable? Does the author give a balanced argument? (see page 57)

7 Create a summary

Creating a summary is a great way to check your understanding of a text. It also makes it easier to remember the main points. You can summarize in different ways based on the type of text. For example:

- **timelines or flow charts**
- **T-charts** (see pages 57 and 102)
- **concept maps** (see page 32)
- **outline summaries** (see page 111)